LIVI
ADVENTU

Sketches from my 'Book of Life'

by Ilse Karger

(Edited by Kurt Strauss)

William Sessions Limited
York, England
1995

© ILSE KARGER

ISBN 1 85072 159 9

'Live adventurously. When choices arise, do you take the way that offers the fullest opportunity for the use of your gifts . . . ?'

Opening part of the ADVICES & QUERIES No. 27 of the Religious Society of Friends (Quakers) in Britain; 1995 Edition.

Printed from Editor's disk
in 10/11 point Plantin Typeface
by William Sessions Limited
The Ebor Press
York, England

CONTENTS

Foreword iv

Introduction v

LIVING ADVENTUROUSLY

Chapter 1   The Early Years   1
Chapter 2   The Twenties and Thirties   19
Chapter 3   America   41
Chapter 4   World War Two and After   57
Chapter 5   Australia   69
Chapter 6   Back to the USA   89
Chapter 7   Life Moves On   103
Chapter 8   A Pilgrimage   117
Chapter 9   Cläre   125
Chapter 10   The Last Chapter   135

SKETCHES FROM MY BOOK OF LIFE

Chapter 11   In Sickness and in Health   147
Chapter 12   Encounters and Relationships   157
Chapter 13   Art, Painting and Poetry   167
Chapter 14   *Geistesgegenwart* and Peak Experiences   183
Chapter 15   Spiritual Insights   193

PHOTOGRAPHS

Hiroshima Day Vigil outside the Minster (York, England, 1984) vi
The Author aged 12 (Berlin, 1914) 10
Student Nurses at the Kaiser Franz Joseph Hospital (Vienna, 1928) 25
At Victor Maxwell House (Sydney, Australia, 1951) 76

Some black-and-white reproductions of the author's many sketches and drawings have also been included. Those dated later than March 1993 were executed after the sudden and unexpected deterioration of her eyesight.

FOREWORD

IN PRAISE OF FRIENDSHIP

TO MY DEAR FRIENDS - friends without whom this book would not have been possible. Your enthusiasm and encouragement held up my spirits after my vision deteriorated so suddenly.

I am blessed to have your friendship, your active help in doing all the typing, all the reading and re-reading the drafts of this book.

It's true that I lived those 93 years — but you re-lived them with me, patiently and with understanding, and so helped me to preserve them.

Kurt Strauss, Barbara Webb and Jane Smedley:

In love and friendship I greet you.

INTRODUCTION

OVER THE LAST FEW YEARS I have been writing down some of my memories, fragments from a long and varied life, and these were published as a series of booklets under the title 'Loose Leaves'. Some of my friends encouraged me to expand these stories into an autobiography. I started to work on this, but all of a sudden my eyesight deteriorated. I found that I could not read any more, not even my own handwriting. I had lost my vision, but found I had very good friends, without whose help this book could not have been written

Why write an autobiography? I am nearing the end of my life. I have no children or grandchildren. What do I have to leave, and to whom can I leave it? My experience in the field of education and human relationships is what I feel I have to offer others. My life has spanned almost the whole of the twentieth century, with all its extraordinary changes. I was nurtured by those changes and I had the opportunity to develop new ideas and put them into practice, so I hand my experience on to future generations. I feel that humanity is one great stream of life, and every generation plays its part in the whole.

In writing about my life I decided early on that this should not take the form of a typical autobiography which describes events in chronological order. Although the first part of this book does describe events in this way, part two contains recollections, thoughts and some poetry as well as providing insights into the spiritual side of my life.

Ilse Karger at the Hiroshima Day Vigil outside the Minster (York, England, 1984)

CHAPTER 1

THE EARLY YEARS

Introducing my parents

MOST PEOPLE THINK that life begins at the point of birth. I feel that the seed to my personality started long before — many of my forefathers have contributed to it, but I know very little about these men and women. I do know that my grandparents on my mother's side got married about the year 1850. The couple had six children (five girls and one boy) but when they were still small, their mother died. The mother's sister lived in New York, and so the brother-in-law asked her to come back to Vienna to take care of his six children and look after his household. She did go back to help; she helped in this way for six years, but then she gave him the choice: "Either you marry me or I leave."

They got married and out of this marriage my mother was born. Mother's oldest sister (half sister) was 22 years older than mother, the youngest 16 years older. Mother grew up like an only child. Two of her sisters were teachers, while the brother studied medicine, later to become an eye surgeon of world renown. Mother herself had a very good education and big aspirations, but at the age of 24 she got married. Why? "All my friends were already married", she told me. " I felt embarrassed. Unmarried girls of my age were looked down upon."

My father, Oskar Karger, who was born in Prussia in 1865, was a widower when he married my mother. His first wife had died a year after they were married, giving birth to their child which had also died.

My parents were both good people, very good people, but their marriage was not a happy one; each of their five children bears witness to that marriage.

1

Mother never had a profession, though she trained as a teacher and had diplomas for teaching French, English and Italian. All her life mother felt bad about being 'only mother and housewife' as she called it. Everything that mother did she did out of a feeling of duty. Duty and discipline were her driving forces. She was very strict, also with herself, and she set very high standards for us.

I was born on the 5th April 1902 in Neu-Ruppin, a town not far from Berlin. I was the second of five children and the first daughter. My first childhood memories are of the time when I was about four years old. My father had a wool shed near the lake shore and sometimes he took me and my younger brother down to the lake with him when he was busy at the wool shed, and while he was working there we would climb around and on and over the big bags of wool, which was a good game for us. Also I remember that he sometimes went fishing at the lake's shore, and we were supplied with some old tin cans and an old spoon and had to dig for worms (*Regenwürmer*) which he used as bait.

Then, in the year 1907, the big move to Berlin came. On the last day in Neu-Ruppin after dinner, each of us was given his or her bottle of milk and told to lie down in one corner of the dining room to drink the milk. There we lay, each in a different corner, flat on our backs, with the bottle of milk. Then the move came. In Berlin we were taken in by the three different sisters of my father for two or three nights, and then we moved into our new flat. When I first entered the new flat, I just stood there in wonder. I couldn't believe it: everything was sparkling; everything was light and bright and white. It was the electric light, which I had never seen before in my life. We also now had central heating, which was something very new to us.

School days and home life

On 1st October 1908 I started my formal education. The class system at that time was very strong; only people who couldn't afford to pay the fees in private schools sent their children to the so-called *Gemeindeschule* - that means only children from the working class, which at that time was really identical with the 'poor' classes, went there.

My first teacher was probably only in her forties, but looked elderly to me. She had greying, straight hair, parted in the middle and put up at the back in a knot. This lady had blue eyes, a very gentle smile on her face. She was soft spoken and I loved her. We started to work through the first reader. On every page was one very nice picture, and underneath one letter, in longhand writing, and every day we studied one page in that reader. Our homework was always to write three lines consisting of this letter, and I loved to do it. I thought school was beautiful, but unfortunately after only two months or even less, this school life came to a sudden end for me, when I came down with measles.

I was made to lie in a darkened room at home for four weeks, which was a very trying and boring time for me. After the four weeks in isolation, it was found that I had a curvature of the spine, and was not allowed to go back to school. I had to start school all over again on 1st April, together with children who were younger than I, and just new in school. Now I was the oldest in the class, but still the shortest by far. The teacher was no longer my beloved Miss Heuser but a youngish woman with reddish hair, a very loud shrieking voice, and a very stern and strict person. This was for me the beginning of a very unhappy time in school. All the years which followed were for me a torment. In the breaks between lessons we were to walk round the edge of the courtyard, two by two. We were not allowed to walk alone, and we were not allowed to walk in threes. I didn't have a friend, but as I wasn't allowed to walk all by myself, I didn't go down to the courtyard: I hid in the toilets, because if a teacher had seen me in the building, I would have been punished.

I was always glad when the bell rang and I could come out of my hiding place and go back into the class, but I was also a very poor pupil. When the teacher called on me to answer a question, I was afraid to answer, in case I would give the wrong answer and she would ridicule me, or show sarcasm, or punish me. Therefore I just froze to stone, and didn't talk at all. I can really say that all through the years I never gave the teacher an answer when I was asked a question. I just stood there and waited until she said: "Sit down." I was good at gym, though, and I loved music and poetry (*more about this in Part II*).

Once I got into a lot of trouble. As we walked to school together, my sister (6) and I (9) stopped at a candy store. I bought fivepence worth of hard candies, and asked to have them put into two separate bags, as I wanted to share them with my sister. My sister asked me: "When shall I eat them?" "Just anytime", I said. Later that morning, when her teacher asked her to read, my sister said: "I cannot read now - I have got something in my mouth." When further questioned, she told her teacher that I had given her the candies and told her to eat them in class. Well, the teacher called for the *Schuldiener* (caretaker). He was sent up to get me out of my classroom in the middle of a lesson and I was brought down before my sister's teacher — it was like a tribunal.

I was not very popular amongst the teachers, but as my written work and my compositions were good, I always passed the examinations, and as my maths was outstanding, I always rose from one class to the next, and so got through the school. But I can't say I was happy there — I was very unhappy.

The atmosphere at home wasn't a very cheerful one either. Before going to school we had to say goodbye to mother. Sometimes when I knocked on mother's door, she would say: "Come in and lock the door." Then she would start crying, and unburden all her unhappiness on to me, telling me about the problems with my father. I listened, but I never said a word. After some time I would look at my watch and say: "Mother, I must go now, otherwise I will be punished for being late for school." Then I would go to school, but would find it difficult to concentrate on my lessons.

There were also other family burdens. As soon as my baby brother started to eat solid food, I more or less became his carer, first feeding him and later telling him stories which I made up specially and which featured him as the main character — a diversion which was to come in useful in later life when I became a teacher. When I became 11 years old, I had to take him (4) and my sister (6) to the park every morning during the school holidays. We would leave the house at 10.00 am with a basket of sandwiches and fruit, overalls and bibs, and were to be back home at 1.45 pm for lunch. It was quite a job to take care of my very lively, even wild, brother. It also became my job to untie the knots in everybody else's shoe laces, and later I became the official family suitcase packer whenever one of the family went somewhere. I must say that my early life provided me with a good basic training in the skills of a carer, which stood me in good stead in later life.

Our family life seemed to be organised around meal times. These were very formal and tense. Father was very impatient, and mother had to serve five children before eating herself. I could never understand why, in a German house, the chamber-maid came in some minutes before the main meal and said, in French: "*Madame est servie.*" Why could she not say: "*Das Essen ist fertig*"? As soon as this was announced, mother would say to us: "Go wash your hands, and go into the dining room." We children

4

had to go into the dining room, stand behind our own chairs, as straight as soldiers, and wait for the arrival of our parents. We wouldn't have dared to sit down until father and mother were seated. The table was always laid very nicely, a big white tablecloth covered the big oak table, and there were always fresh flowers in the middle. Father, as the head of the family, sat at the head of the table, in a chair which was his chair. The 'father's chair' at that time, in the so-called upper middle class, was designed a little differently from all the other dining room chairs. It had a higher back, and arms at the sides. The chamber-maid served the dinner. Father was served first, then the platters were put next to mother, who served all of us.

Mother was very anxious about good table manners, and we children were not allowed to talk at the table unless we were asked a question by the parents, but you could hear mother say: "Take your elbow off the table!" "Hold your knife properly!" "Sit up straight!" "Your index finger doesn't belong on that side of the knife! Put it back." We had to eat up what mother served up on the plate; we were not allowed to leave anything.

In our sitting room on the wall hung a still-life which my mother had painted as a young girl. It was a very good painting. A smaller painting hung in the dining room, of a skull with a twig of dead leaves in a toothless mouth. In my view it did not belong in the dining room; it did not do anything to improve one's appetite.

In the mornings, we children had breakfast under the supervision of the governess. Each of us had to drink at least one cup of milk and eat one whole roll with butter. The rolls were cut into two halves and quite often when I returned from school at dinner time, mother asked me: "Did you eat all your roll this morning for breakfast?" and if the answer was "No, I only ate half of it" then I had to eat the other half right before I could start my dinner. Sometimes it happened that I didn't come home in time for dinner. If I had hurried straight back from school, I could have been there in time, at 2.00 o'clock, but on the way home I often stopped. If I saw a pram on the other side of the street I went across to have a look at the baby, or I would stop in the park and play marbles by myself for a little while, or if I hadn't eaten my sandwich for elevenses I would stop on the way to feed it to a horse, as I didn't dare to bring it back home. When I came home, and the family was already eating the main course, mother would say: "You are late again. No dessert for you today. Go and ask Emma to heat up the soup for you." Of course children didn't argue with their parents. I didn't say anything, but inside myself I thought: 'That doesn't make sense to me. That isn't very logical. What I should be missing is the soup, which has been carried out of the dining room already. The dessert hasn't been served yet. Why do I have to miss that?'

We didn't do any entertaining at home, nor did we go out to any parties, but sometimes I was invited to a birthday party by one of the children in my class, though she wasn't a special friend of mine. I didn't want to go to those birthday parties but my mother forced me to go. She would buy me a present to take along, and send me off. I would go, but not happily, as I wasn't conditioned to be among cheerful, happy people. I would sit at the birthday table there, drink my hot chocolate, eat my piece of cake quietly, and then as soon as some of the adults sat at the piano to organize games or singing, I started to cry. I went out into the hall, put on my coat and went home. I could not stand any cheerful people around me.

Also at home, being the oldest daughter (we were three boys and two girls) I had to help clean up after the boys because in Germany at that time men and boys had no duties in the home at all; not only that but they were not <u>allowed</u> to move a finger. They were trained to be waited on by their sisters, and that of course meant that in later life they expected to be waited on by their wives. A German man was never seen with a pram in the street, or carrying a package; that was beneath his dignity.

On vacation

I was already ten years old when I had my first vacation. The year before, mother took the two elder boys to the country to see if she could manage. After two or three weeks she came back with the two boys and said: "Awful! Never again will I go with children into a hotel. Impossible!" So the following spring mother and father went away for a few days together to see if they could find a suitable place for the whole family. I must say they were very lucky and they came back full of enthusiasm that they had found the right place. This time it was going to be a real vacation, in the mountains, in a peasant's house.

When summer came, off we went - the whole family, father, mother, the five children, a household help, and some big trunks with all the household wares. We took along sheets and bedding, pots and pans -

everything that was needed for the household. It was a very long trip on the train. We had rented a whole compartment for our family. We left Berlin in the morning at eight o'clock and in the afternoon about four o'clock we arrived at our destination. That is to say, we had not yet arrived at our destination but this was the terminus for the train and the last part of the trip had to be done by *Kramsa*. This was something like an old-fashioned bus drawn by two horses. We all got on board and off we went to Ruston. It was quite an interesting trip, up and down through the mountains and forests and small villages. Finally we arrived at Ruston. It was not a village; it was smaller than a village. It consisted of five peasant houses, which had no relationship to each other, each one standing isolated in a meadow in a narrow valley surrounded by beautiful forests.

We were to stay in a peasant house which had three entrance doors at the front. The first entrance was for people. The second entrance, looking just the same, went straight into the stable, where we saw six or eight cows and some calves. The third door went into what was called the *Scheune*, which was a shelter for three goats, and home for a whole flock of chickens. Under the roof of the peasant house were several swallows' nests, and we children enjoyed watching the swallows flying out and coming back into the nests to feed their young ones. For us children Ruston was heaven. Here we were really in the country enjoying the fresh meadows with the wild flowers. We watched the peasant cut the grass, we helped to rake the hay and we also helped clean the cow shed. As a matter of fact my younger brother and sister were always fighting about who cleaned out more of the cow shed.

I enjoyed watching the peasant woman sitting on her milking stool and sometimes I was even allowed to try to milk a cow. It was music in my ears to hear the fresh milk flowing into the milk bucket. The peasant woman baked her own bread of course, and made her own butter, and we enjoyed having this very good wholemeal bread, fresh butter, fresh milk, potatoes and vegetables. In the forest we collected blueberries, which were there in masses, and we also sometimes looked for mushrooms. There was a special treat when we found enough *Pfefferlinge* (that is a certain kind of mushroom which only grows in Germany, and they are a real delicacy) to have a whole meal of them.

We went to Ruston many years in succession - Ruston was our summer vacation for at least six or seven summers. When finally the day came when we had to board the train to go back to Berlin and to school, we were all very sad, and as the train pulled into Berlin and we saw the big blocks of flats and the large windows, we were in tears. Not that life was always confined to the city, though. For about a year, my sister and I belonged to a Jewish hiking club (none of the others would have us as members) and those outings, particularly in springtime, were really enjoyable. We would all meet somewhere in the morning with our knapsack and a picnic lunch, and then we would walk and sing to the music of the guitars which our leaders played. In fact, even on my way to school I would sometimes sing folk songs and 'walking songs'.

Christmas time

One of the highlights of my childhood every year was Christmas. It began with 'Nikolaus', the feast of St. Nicholas. On the 5th December, before going to bed, we put one of our shoes on the window sill, and then, early in the morning — sometimes even in the night — we tiptoed to the window in the dark. Good Nikolaus never disappointed us: we always found our shoes filled. They had actually been extended with white paper cuffs where the socks should go, and in these were all kinds of good things: nuts, raisins, dates, chocolates, marzipan — the shoes were filled right to the brim.

Christmas itself was something very special. Weeks beforehand you smelled the different cookies, biscuits, and cakes which were being baked. We children always made some presents for our parents. We would never have given them a bought present - presents had to be made and secretly worked on for many weeks. When finally Christmas came, the French doors connecting the living and dining rooms were locked, and mother

8

was busy setting up everything for Christmas in the living room. There was always a very large tree and of course it had real candles and was hung not only with lametta and artificial decorations but mainly with things to eat - small red-cheeked apples, mandarins, biscuits like chocolate stars, and little baskets with hazel nuts and walnuts, raisins, dates, chocolate and marzipan.

On Christmas Eve in the evening we all lined up and waited in the dining room, each one with a present for the parents. When the French doors were opened it was like paradise. There was that beautiful, big, decorated tree in the corner of the living room and in the middle was a big, long, table, with a white cloth, and there were all the presents. Everyone of us children was shown his or her place where his or her presents were all arranged like a display in a toy store. There was also, at every place, a so-called '*bunter Teller*'. This was a big plate full of things to eat - an orange or an apple and marzipan and cookies and raisins and dates and chocolate - everything you could think of. There was also a nice Christmas cake at each place which was individually baked for each child. Then after looking at all the presents we would have the traditional dinner — carp fish with raisin sauce and all the trimmings which traditionally went with it. As a dessert we were allowed to go and take something from the tree, which was a special treat also. Then, as bedtime came, each of us was allowed to take one present into bed.

The next morning, Christmas Day, we usually took a walk, either with the new doll in our arms, or the new doll's carriage, and you saw in the street all the children with their new toys, which was always very nice to see. So Christmas was really a day of love and happiness. Everybody was joyful - everybody was happy - everybody had presents for everybody else and got presents from everybody else.

When I was about 10 years old, my mother would come and say goodnight to my sister and me, who shared a room. My mother went to my sister's bed and kissed her 'goodnight'. Then mother, on her way out of the door, would call over to me 'goodnight' and I would be in tears for

The author aged 12 (Berlin, 1914)

a long time. Some months later I invented a game. Every evening after my mother had said 'goodnight' I became my own infant. I would put myself into a nice baby pram, onto a soft feather-filled mattress. I would rock the baby lovingly, stroke its cheek tenderly and say 'sleep well'. And so, with my thumb in my mouth, I — the baby — would fall asleep.

I think my worst time, the time of utter loneliness, was between the ages of 14 and 16. I felt desolate and lost. At night, when everybody was sleeping, I would get up, sit at the table, and write stories and poetry with tears running down my cheeks. 'Here I am', I would think, 'belonging to a large family, and nobody knows what I am doing — how I am feeling.' In the early morning hours I would tear up what I had written, and go back to my bed and sleep. In the morning at 6.30 my mother would have a hard time to wake me up. "You don't get enough sleep", she would say, "You must go to bed earlier! Eight-thirty is too late for you."

Then my unhappiness came to a head. When I was about 15, this thought came to me: 'If I really wanted to die, could I just lie down and die? Could I just will my body to lay down and die? Without using any force, without opening gas taps or taking an overdose of pills, or cutting my wrist or jumping out of the window?' I really wanted to know what I could do with my will-power, and I would try it out.

That evening, as I lay in bed, I thought: 'I want to be ill. I want to be really ill.' I concentrated on the wish to be ill, and with that wish I went to sleep. In the middle of the night I woke up with cramps. I felt just awful. Everything inside me hurt. I felt miserable, really miserable.

Next morning at 6.30 my mother came into my room as usual to wake me up, and tell me it was time to get dressed and ready for school. "I can't go to school, mother. I can't get up; I'm not well." "What's wrong with you?" asked my mother. "I don't know, but I feel awful." "Do you have a sore throat?" "No." "Do you have 'flu?" "No, I don't have 'flu." "Do you have a temperature?" "No." And mother said: "All right, if you refuse to get up, and think you are ill, I will have to call the doctor." So the general practitioner was called.

He came, and looked into my throat. No sore throat. He felt my glands. Nothing wrong with the glands. He took my temperature. "Oh yes, she's got a high temperature." He started to test my abdomen. "Oh! Oh!" I said. "It hurts awfully." "Yes", said the doctor, "I can see that."

His diagnosis was: "There is an acute inflammation of the intestines, but on a nervous basis. I'm sorry, but it will take about 8 to 10 days. She has to stay in bed until it wears off." I for my part was as happy as a lark, because it had proved for me that my will-power was very strong, that it was up to me to decide whether I wanted to be alive or not, and that gave me a very good feeling. In fact, after that experience I never felt so unhappy again, because I felt I had control over my own life.

World War I

It is 80 years ago now that the first World War started, but I still have very vivid memories of that time. Of our immediate family, no one was called into active service. My father was too old at 49, and my brothers were too young; the oldest was 13. The war nevertheless interrupted our daily routine, at home as well as in school. Pretty soon the food started to be short, and ration cards were given out to everyone. These covered meat, vegetables, butter, cheese and eggs.

Clothes were also rationed. Children could get only one pair of new trousers, or a set of underwear, or shoes, each year. For growing boys one pair of trousers was not really sufficient - if one needed an extra pair, one had to go to the magistrate's office and make a case for having a second pair. As the food became more and more scarce, substitutes began to appear on the market, for instance egg substitute made from some chemical, and when these too ran out, a substitute appeared for the substitute. I remember asking my mother to try to get the 'real substitute', because the other tasted too awful.

Every person was allowed one loaf of bread a week; as the flour got short, the bakers started to mix in some sawdust, wood shavings, and when the public complained, the newspaper ran an article saying that the health authorities had carried out research on wood shavings, and had found that these were not bad for your health. They didn't claim the shavings had any health value, merely that they weren't dangerous, so the bakers were allowed to put them in. Leather shoes were unobtainable, and we wore shoes with soles of thick wood, and the uppers like cardboard or papier maché. They were coloured black, and looked like black Oxford shoes, but in winter, when it snowed, the snow stuck under the soles like a cradle, and every so often we had to stop and knock the compacted snow off the soles.

The food rations we could buy with the cards were pretty low anyway but the cards were no guarantee that one would receive one's entitlement; often it simply wasn't in the shops. A routine developed of queuing up in front of the shop early in the morning for butter, margarine, or a little piece of cheese, and two of us children would go down and start queueing at 6.30 or 7.00 o'clock, and when it was time for us to go to school, my mother and the cook would take our places. We stood four in a row, and the shop let in about 12 people at a time. It was always very annoying when, after we had stood there for two or three hours and our row finally got to the front, a sign was put outside the door saying 'Closed', because they had run out of merchandise.

As the magistrate's office for rationing was near my school, it was always my job to go there whenever one of us, for example my youngest brother, needed new shoes or trousers badly. I had to try to get a form for him to fill in, and that was not a very pleasant job; you really had to beg, and convince them how urgent it was. There was a shortage of teachers too; many young teachers had gone off to fight, so the classes were joined together and instead of 40 pupils in a class, there were 50 or even 60. As coal became scarce, the schools were no longer fully heated either, or not heated at all.

At the beginning of the war, when Hindenburg (who soon became a hero) marched into Russia with his troops, there was a so-called victory announced every other day, or at least once a week. Whenever another Russian town fell, it was celebrated as a big victory all over Germany. The next day we were sent home from school to celebrate, and we sang '*Heil Dir im Siegerkranz*' and '*Deutschland, Deutschland über alles*' and other nationalistic songs in the school assembly hall. Students and others were encouraged to become more and more patriotic; we school children were told that the English and the French were our enemies, our worst enemies, and we had to hate them with all our hearts and all our minds; they were robbers and thieves. At the same time we were expected to study their languages, and I couldn't see any reason for that. If the English people were so awful, and since I never expected in my life to visit England, why bother to learn English? I also knew that I would never ever live in America, so again: why learn English? I didn't want to learn things that would be of no use to me.

At the beginning of the war we had a big map of Germany and its borders, hanging in the entrance hall of our flat, and we had lots of pins with the German flag, the eagle, on them. Every morning, when the

Berliner Tagesblatt was brought in, my brothers would assemble round the newspaper, and the first thing that was done was to see where the German army was. "Look! Yesterday they were there. Today they are already further in Russia. Let's move the pins to show the advance." Then the paper was opened, and one of my brothers found the list of soldiers who were the victims, or as the paper put it, the heroes, who had been killed. One took a deep breath and said: "Thank God, no one from our immediate family, or related to us, or personally known to us, has been killed." Then one looked at the list of those missing. Again a deep breath. No one we knew. I don't know why, but I never felt comfortable at this. I always felt it was just as bad if it was someone we didn't know; those soldiers too had parents who missed them, were worried about them; they too had young wives or other relatives. I couldn't see why we should be glad, just because there was no one that we knew.

It was the same with food: my father had contacts with farms through his business, and knew a lot of farmers. Sometimes they sent us some sausage, or cold cuts of meat, or a whole ham. Once we received a package with fresh fish (or rather, it was fresh when it had been sent, but it spent too long travelling and when it arrived it was no longer fresh). This was in 1917; food was very very short, and we were very hungry, but my father advised us not to eat it. The decision was left to us, however. We all ate it, except my father ... and we all got very sick with food poisoning, which it took us a long time to get over.

Milk too was very short; only children under six were entitled to a quarter litre, and in our family only one child qualified, so that was what our family received each day. As for clothes, there was no material to make dresses, and certainly nothing ready made. People started making dresses out of curtains, and I remember that my mother had some large flannel petticoats in her hope chest which she had never worn. She dyed them navy blue and had dresses made out of them for my sister and me. We wore these for several years, and loved them. We still remember them as being amongst the nicest we ever had.

After the war was over and food was again obtainable, I remember that we didn't eat as much or as well as my mother thought we should. "It's here on the table, and available for everyone. Why don't you eat?" I felt that my stomach had got used to only a little food, and couldn't deal with normal portions or rich food any more. It took a long time to adjust to 'normality' again. In fact, things never did get back to 'normal', ie what things were like before the war. One never really had the feeling that there was peace again, that there would be no more war. A sort of cold war continued; I always had the feeling that the German people only had one thought: "Let's build up and become strong again so that we can take revenge." The German people never admitted that they had lost the war. I remember that we were told in school: "We didn't lose the war. The German soldiers are the best soldiers in the world, the bravest, the most courageous. The only reason we didn't win was that the English didn't play fair."

Professional training

In April 1919 I was finished with my so-called school education. Mother suggested that I go to a *Haushaltungsschule* to learn sewing. I protested: "I don't have to learn that", and I was going to prove it. I bought a piece of white linen material. I designed a pretty nightgown and sewed it all by hand. It really was a work of art. It had a V-neck, shoulder panels, made of lace (filet), pleats at the waistline on each side, at the bottom a hand-sewn hem with drawn threads. When it was all finished I modelled the nightdress for my mother to see. She looked at it critically. "Isn't it pretty?" I said. "Yes, it is pretty." "Doesn't it fit well?" "Yes, it fits well", and then mother said sternly, "But it is not a nightie, it is a dress!"

What now? I was determined to have a profession. But which? I suggested working in a florist's shop, arranging flower displays, at which I was very good. My father said: "No. Ridiculous. Out of the question." Then I suggested becoming a paediatrician. "No", said my father, "No. As a doctor you would have to get up at night to make night calls. That is out." My third suggestion was nursery school teacher. "Do you want to wipe the dirty noses of other people's children?" said my father in disgust. "The only honourable profession for a girl from a good family is house-daughter. Stay at home and help your mother."

Protective custody! My father's idea was that the man was the head of the family: the ruler, the voice of the family. The wife was his treasured possession (MY wife, MY daughter, MY son). My mother's idea was to give the children as good an education as possible, then let them become independent. Mother was a democrat in theory, but not in practice. "Don't sit on that chair like a servant", she would say if I happened to sit on the edge of the chair. "Behave yourselves; you're not children of the street."

My mother was of the opinion that I should aim for a profession, but not that of nursery school teacher. When I asked her why not, she said: "You only want to become a nursery school teacher because you like children, but that isn't a good reason. You ought to find a profession which you think you will not like to do, because that is the only way to practise self-discipline." "No, mother", I said, "I don't think so. I think one ought to enter a profession that one likes. Problems will come up by themselves in any profession; you don't have to make them for yourself before you start." And so I began training as a kindergarten teacher.

At the end of the course came the time of my state exams, and it was a very difficult one, to say the least. My mother had gone off to Vienna, as she had done several times before, claiming to proceed with a divorce. The atmosphere at home was a very heavy one. I had to supervise the running of the household and plan the family meals, while at the same time preparing for all my exams. Then I received a letter from mother saying: 'I will come back home. Father promised ....' I wrote to mother: 'If you want to come back only because father promised this and that, then do not come back, as father never keeps his promises'. Mother sent my letter to my father, and he confronted me with it. "That is the most brutal thing that a daughter could do to her father", he said, and told me to leave his house.

The following morning I asked the director of the college if I could be a boarder there for the week of the exams. But when I told my father that I would stay at the college for the week of the state exams, he decreed: "You are staying at home, where you belong - and I want you at home tomorrow in time for dinner at 2.00pm." "I cannot - I will have exams all day. I will be home after 7.00pm." "I do not care about your exams! You do not need to take them." The next morning at 6.30 the maid knocked at my door: "Your father wants to see you before you leave the house", she said. All ready to leave, I went to see my father. "When will you come home?" he asked. "At 7.00 o'clock." "You will be home before 2.00 o'clock for dinner." "Father, I cannot." "Then you are not going!" Father jumped out of bed, ran out into the hall and locked the front door. I ran through the kitchen to the back door, and walked down the winding iron stairs from the third to the ground floor. An hour later I sat for my first exam.

I was poor in all the theoretical exams, but on the strength of my 'working with the group of children' I passed. We got our assignments by drawing lots. Mine was a group of 20 children, boys and girls aged 4 to 12, and I had to organize a project with them as a group activity. All the children were strangers to me. We met for half an hour before the examining body (about 10 people) walked in on us, pads and pens in hand. When I had met the children, shaking hands with them in greeting, one of the 12-year-old boys said to me: "Miss, you don't have to be scared. We won't let you fail. We will behave", and right away I felt myself part of a team with these children, the so-called under-privileged children from the slums of Berlin.

Soon after the exams were over I went to a training school which taught arts and crafts for six months, and after that I started my first private nursery school. A family provided an empty room in their flat, and in exchange for that, their two children didn't have to pay anything. I did not feel that I could manage more than eight children all together - it was a kind of make-shift arrangement, but the children and their parents were happy, and I carried on for quite a while. Sadly, nobody in my family understood my interest in children. They called it *Kinderkwatsch* or child-nonsense. One of the mothers, whose children belonged to my nursery school, said to me one day: "I wish people could see you with the children. You are so different, so relaxed, so cheerful and happy. Why are you so stern and sharp when you are with the adults?" "That is my only weapon", I said. "Why do you need a weapon?" she asked. 'Perhaps', I thought, 'It was as a result of the atmosphere in which I grew up at home and in school.'

During the summer vacation, to my father's annoyance, I took a job as a governess, accompanying a family with two difficult children to a summer resort. The second summer I went with those two children alone, so as to give the mother a chance to go to a clinic for treatment. I had a good friendly relationship with that family till the end of their lives — they all perished in a concentration camp.

———

World War I had ended in 1918, but the scars that were left were very deep. Things seemed to go from bad to worse. Inflation! What inflation! The value of the German Mark changed every day. One million Marks did not even buy a day's food! Of course we had the 'revolution', which brought many good things in its wake, women's liberation for instance. The women had proved during the war that they could, and indeed did, replace men everywhere: as bus drivers, as machinists, as factory workers, etc. But all this was overshadowed by the inflation. Rich people became poor overnight as the value of the money changed every

17

day at noon. As soon as your wages were paid, you ran to town to spend it, as it would be worth less the next day. In 1923 I too was a 'multi-millionaire'. In normal times the children paid 20 Marks per month. Now I made it the value of four loaves of bread on the day the fees were paid for one week.

I ran that private nursery school under very difficult conditions for two years. Then, in the Autumn of 1924, I took a job with a married couple, a neurologist and a paediatrician. The paediatrician had been one of my teachers in the social pedagogic seminar, and she offered me a job in her house for six weeks to replace her assistant nurse and receptionist who had gone on vacation. She and her husband, the neurologist, had their surgery in the same flat, and shared the same waiting room for their patients. For me it was a very happy and fruitful time. I learnt a lot as I answered the phone and the door, made appointments, cooked dinner for the family and in the evening helped their daughter with her French homework.

One day as I opened the front door I faced a young woman whom I knew, Grete Hoffmann. I had been sitting next to her for eight years in my class at school, but we had never talked with each other beyond saying good morning when we came into the class and goodbye at the end of the day. I liked Grete; she was a nice quiet girl. I knew she came from a big family with five children, like my family. She was pale and timid, with big black eyes and looked a little sad. I always wished that she would approach me, but didn't dare to talk to her.

That day, when I opened the door for her, I just ushered her into the waiting room, offered her a seat, and left her. That evening, when I sat at the dinner table with the doctor and his family, he said to me: "Ilse, there was someone here today who knew you." I said: "Grete Hoffmann", and told him how I felt about her, had always felt about her. He said: "Just exactly what you told me about her is what she told me about you." How sad, how very sad, I thought, that neither of us had made the first step to a closer relationship. We could have been good friends.

CHAPTER 2

THE TWENTIES AND THIRTIES

My first visit to Vienna

IT WAS RIGHT AFTER CHRISTMAS 1925. My aunt had just lost her husband and lived by herself in a big 6-room flat with two servants. She invited me to visit her for some weeks, and so I went off to Vienna. The next day already I realised that my aunt, a society lady, had bridge parties scheduled at least three to four times a week, and so I thought it would be a good idea for me to try to get into the hospital as a voluntary worker to learn something about sick children as a supplementary training to my profession as kindergarten teacher.

The next day I went off to see the chief doctor of the children's department of the Kaiser Franz Josef Hospital, a big state hospital in Vienna. When I asked Prof. Reuss if he could take me on as a voluntary helper, he said: "No, I don't like voluntary workers." I asked him why not? His answer was: "I have had bad experiences with voluntary workers." I asked why? "They are not dependable", he said, "They come and go as they please. Because they are not paid, they feel they are free to do what they want." I said that I would be dependable. He said: "How often would you like to come?" "Every day; six days a week." "What hours would you like to work?" "What times do the nurses work?" "The nurses are all nuns", he said, "They start work at 7.00 in the morning." "Then I will be here at 7.00 o'clock every morning also."

"And how long would you like to stay every day?" "Would it be alright if I stayed until 4.00 in the afternoon?" "Yes" he said, "That would be all right, but if you are here from 7.00 in the morning till 4.00 in the afternoon, we should at least give you a hot dinner at noon, but since all the nurses are nuns, we would have a problem. Not being a nun, you couldn't eat in the dining room with them. I'd have to talk with the Mother Superior and see if we can make some arrangement for you." They did make an arrangement. The next Monday morning at 7.00 o'clock I was there, ready to work.

At 12.00 o'clock one of the nuns came into the ward where I was busy feeding one of the infants and said: "Now you have to come and have your dinner. Come with me." I went with the nun down a long long corridor. She opened a door into what seemed to be a very narrow room. As she went in sideways she seemed to cover something with her big skirt which she spread out as she walked. There was a small table laid for me, with a white napkin spread on it, and nice clean covered dishes with the food. She made me sit down, facing a white wall, and wished me a good appetite and left the room. I wondered what she was trying to hide behind me as I entered the room. I turned my head, and there to my surprise was a big bath tub. Apparently this was the bathroom; they didn't have any other room where they could serve me, and so for the next four weeks I always had my solitary dinner in that little bathroom.

I worked in that department for a whole month, and after the month was up my aunt said to me: "You haven't really seen much of Vienna, or had much pleasure out of being here, leaving the house at 6.00 in the morning and coming back after 5.00 in the evening. How would you like to stay another month?" I thought it over, and then said: "Yes, I would love to stay longer, but under one condition. That you allow me to go to a cookery school, and to learn cooking while I am here in Vienna." So for the next three weeks I went twice a week to a private cookery school.

———

After that I returned to Berlin, and got a job as a group worker in a home for problem children. It was run by the state, and the children were sent there by the social welfare department. Some were taken from their family home, because the home didn't look after them well, or they had been in trouble with the law and had been sent by the courts. It was located in the country, and we had over 100 children of all ages, from toddlers upwards. I worked with a group of school-children aged 8 - 10. Our house had a large garden, at the end of which was the river Elbe. We used this for bathing, and the children very much enjoyed bathing in the summer. I was very happy working in that home, but after six months it was closed for financial reasons.

Italy

In February 1926 I took on a job in Italy as governess to a Count's children; in winter in Turin, in summer in the family's own castle in the country. Full of expectation, but without any knowledge of the Italian language, I left Berlin. I carried with me a small booklet called 'The most essential sentences to travel in Italy'.

My first stop was Milan, where after a long and tiring journey the train finally arrived. As the train pulled in to the station I leaned out of the window, in my hand my little Italian booklet. I called out: "*Fachino, Fachino!*" The *Fachino* (porter) came. "*Una valigia da conservare*", I told him (a suitcase for the Left Luggage Office). The porter looked at me and laughed heartily. I said it once more and he laughed even more. I then showed him my booklet. I let him read it for himself. He could not stand up straight, he laughed so much. But as we walked through the station I found the place to deposit my luggage. The next thing was to find a taxi. I did not see any, so I got a *Droschke* (a horse drawn carriage) to take me to relations of an uncle of mine. They had kindly invited me to stay for some days.

After what seemed a very long ride through Milan we finally arrived there. I walked up the four flights and rang the bell. An elderly lady opened the door and greeted me in French. It gave me a shock. It shocked me into talking French. I had not known that my hostess was French. She did not speak German. When later she asked me: "Where did you learn to talk French so well?" my answer was: "In your house" (I had taken up French in school, but had never spoken it).

Two days later I went on to Turin. The Contessa met me at the station. She addressed me in German, and as we walked out of the station she said: "We will take a *Droschke*, not a taxi. That will take longer to get home and I will have more time to talk to you. There are three things that you must know before we get home, three unpleasant things. First: I have four children, not two as I told you in my letter. But the two older boys, 14 and 15, have nothing to do with you. Second: I hope you are not afraid of dogs; we have a big German police dog. He is very vicious. Only yesterday he bit our new chambermaid so badly that I had to take the poor thing to the hospital. I will let the dog wear a muzzle for the first week that you are in the house. Only the trouble is that he can take it off himself. I will give you a white apron to wear. Then the dog might think that you are the nurse and might not bite you."

"The third thing, which may be the worst", the Contessa continued, "is that the infant's nurse, whom we have had for three years, is still here; she refused to leave. She wants to be sure that you are nice enough with Roberto, the three year old child. Of course, I could not take the room away from Sister Rosa. I must ask you to sleep in a very small room temporarily. But this room is next to the dining room, and Happy the dog sleeps in the dining room. In the morning you must stay in your little room until I come and get you. If you come out alone, the dog will surely bite you."

Well, this was my reception! That first night I felt like a prisoner in solitary confinement. I could not even go to the toilet. And it was not the end of my difficulties. In the morning the Contessa came into my room. She seemed very agitated. "I must ask you something. It's very embarrassing", she said. "You are not by any chance Jewish, are you?" "I am Jewish." "Oh", said the Contessa, "That we must not tell my husband. He would never allow his children to be educated by a Jew." "I can leave", I said. " There is not any bond between us yet; we are still strangers to each other." The Contessa replied: "But I would feel awful! What would your family think of us if we sent you back home." "I am not a practising Jew, but I am a Jew and will never deny I am Jew." "The Count must give his approval." The next day the Count asked me to stay, and I stayed on for two very happy years.

For the first week I let Sister Rosa take care of Roberto. I just stood by quietly outside, but at times I felt quite shocked inside. Roberto was handled and treated like an infant and behaved like an infant; he actually acted as if he was a baby. He acted it very well. Roberto got washed and dressed on top of the bathonette. He reached out for his shoes and dropped them down on to the floor. Sister Rosa picked them up. I looked at her somewhat surprised, and she said: "He is a Count's child." At the breakfast table, this Count's child took his cup, the full cup, and turned it upside down on to the table cloth, and Sister Rosa explained: "He does that always. It means that he does not want to drink his milk." Roberto, or Tini as he was called, was a late-born child. For the family he was 'the baby'. The Contessa regarded him almost as her lapdog. "Come here, Tini", she would say, "Sit on my lap and let me kiss you."

Here I was in a strange world, very different from what I was used to. And the customs in this family! When I asked for a towel, the Contessa explained: "We all use the same towel, a clean one every day." The family also shared one hairbrush and one comb - the Count had his own living quarters. At the dinner table everything was very formal. The food was served on large silver platters by a waitress with white gloves. We spoke in four languages. The Count in English to me, the Contessa French, Julia, the thirteen year old, in German, and Tini a mixture of German and Italian. The family spoke Italian amongst themselves. Italian was music to my ears; I loved to listen to it. Twice a week Julia gave me an Italian lesson and twice a week I gave her one in German.

Some words about the Contessa. She was of French noblesse, good looking, very charming, friendly and good natured. The Count, on his father's side, was from an old Italian family. He owned that beautiful old castle, which had been in the family's possession for a thousand years. All summer the family lived in that castle. On his mother's side the Count was a grandson of the German musicians Robert and Clara Schumann. Incidentally Happy, the vicious dog, never bit me or anybody else while I was there. He was my constant companion, day and night. He even shared my bed.

Austria again

I had to leave Italy for health reasons. In October 1927 I went back to Berlin. The next months were very painful for me, in different ways. Then I received a letter from Prof. Reuss under whom I had worked as a volunteer in the Kaiser Franz Josef Hospital in Vienna, saying that he was going to start a private nursing school in the hospital. He asked whether I would be interested in joining as a student, and take the diploma examination at the end of the course.

Though I wasn't at all well and in a lot of pain, I decided to accept the offer, feeling that nothing could happen to me there, since I would already be in hospital and they would take care of me. Instead of going to a sanatorium for six weeks, as the Berlin doctor had advised me to do, I entered the training school for nursing. The course was supposed to last for one year. We began on 1st January 1928, and it was really a very good course. The school being in the grounds of the big General Hospital, we had the opportunity to work in all fields of nursing, and we saw and learnt a lot. Here again, though, I felt quite isolated. I didn't really fit into that group.

I was the only German; all the others were Austrian. I was the oldest, aged 26; the others were 18 and 19. I was the only Jew; all the others were Protestants. But we learnt a lot. The very first day when we started, the professor called me into his office and said: "Ilse, you are a nursery school teacher and *Hortnerin*. I am going to take advantage of you. I want you to start something (which nowadays would be called occupational therapy)." This technique wasn't known at that time, but he began to introduce it through me. He gave me some money to buy whatever material I needed, and sent me to town to get it. "For the next two weeks, in the mornings, I want you to go from bed to bed, and give every child who doesn't have a high temperature something to do. The first week you will do it alone. The second week I want you to take along one of your colleagues and show her how to do it - how to keep the children occupied and happy. For the next student it will be the first week with you, under your guidance, and her second week she will train the next one. In this way, the children will be occupied all through the year, and all the student nurses will have learnt how to occupy sick children in bed."

It worked very well. We found very soon that the children not only looked better, but ate better, and got well faster. The professor, who had very good and modern ideas, was modernising the whole children's department and we, the students, were his tools. We didn't have a very easy time carrying out his progressive orders because we had to work under the nuns, and the nuns didn't like our modern ways. For instance, they didn't want us to undress the children and do gym with them while they were in the nude; they wanted them to be fully dressed.

When the time came for me to work for one week under the Sister in charge of the Out Patient Department, good luck was with me again. After I had worked there for four days as a student nurse, the Sister fell sick, and I was told to carry on on my own. I liked the feeling of being in charge of the department. It was a very good practice for me, being the only nurse working there and helping four doctors. I had to receive the patients, to admit them and to weigh them, and do all that before the doctor saw the children. I had to treat little sores and wounds, I had to put ointment and bandages on, and I had to be pretty fast to keep up with the demands of the four doctors.

I was allowed to carry on in the Out Patient Department for children for three weeks, and I really enjoyed it. Once, all of us ten student nurses got scabies, which one of us had brought home from the beach. We were all put into isolation for over a week, I think. We were told to sacrifice one of our garments, underwear shirt and underwear panties, as we had to be treated with a black heavy ointment from the neck down to

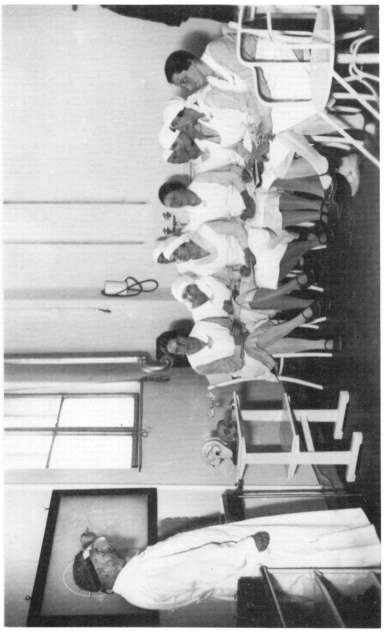

Student nurses at the Kaiser Franz Joseph Hospital; the author is on the extreme right (Vienna, 1928)

25

the toes, so we all sat together, huddled up in front of the electric fire, on a mat. The professor didn't want us to lose any time on the lectures, so all the lectures were given to us in our dormitory, in front of the electric stove. In the evening the professor himself came with his violin and gave us nice concerts in order to raise our spirits.

During this year Helen, one of my colleagues, contracted diphtheria. She died, and the day after her death I found myself sick with diphtheria in the same little room in which she had died. I felt very weak and oh-so-tired, but did not sleep all night. A nun, one of the nursing staff, said to me: "Helen was also very tired and could not fall asleep. But then one day she did fall asleep and did not wake up any more. Why don't you try to do the same?"

At the end of the year we had the exams, all written, and then we received our diplomas as trained nurses for sick infants and children up to 14, after which I returned to Berlin.

Back in Berlin

On the evening I arrived back, my mother said: "Elizabeth, our maid, isn't feeling very well, so I sent her to bed after lunch, and gave her something to gargle. I told her that if she didn't feel well in the night, she should knock at your door for help."

Before I went to bed, I thought I'd go and have a look at Elizabeth, so I went up to her room and chatted with her. Just as I was about to leave the room, she gave out one cry. "You aren't going to have a baby, are you?" I asked her, and she said: "Yes, I think I am." I lifted up her blanket, and sure enough, the baby was on the way. I got a bucket of warm water, scissors, silk thread and so on, locked the door, and started to busy myself as a midwife. We had been told in the nursing class that we were only allowed to deliver a baby in cases of emergency, when there wasn't time to get help. Here was an emergency. It was a normal, easy birth — a big healthy baby boy. While I was attending to the young mother and her baby, everybody in the house was getting excited.

My mother called up our family doctor, who told her to call up the Fire Department, as in Berlin it was the job of the Fire Department to respond to every kind of emergency. My father walked up and down the long hall and in a sorrowful voice he said: "This is the worst thing that

26

could have happened in a house where there are two grown-up daughters." And then, through the closed door, father advised me: "Do not touch that baby, you could hurt him." Then my brother came to the door: "Don't bath the baby, you could burn him." My other brother: "What can we give him to eat? The baby will be very hungry."

When I asked my mother how I could dispose of the afterbirth, mother got very irritated. "I don't want to hear anything about it", she said. "But mother, you have had five children!" And her answer to this was: "In my time that was different. One lay between silk comforters and saw nothing at all." Then the doorbell rang; two firemen came in. They put Elizabeth on a stretcher and put her baby into her arms, and thanked me for having done their job.

Back to Austria

In 1929 I was back in Vienna, where I had taken on a job as sister in charge of the Open Air Department of a private children's convalescent home: the *Sängerwarte*. It was owned and run by Dr Robert, a paediatrician. I was told I would be in charge of 20 children (ages 2-12) and have a young helper. When I got there I found that the youngest child in my group was an infant of six months, and the young helper a little girl of 14 years. She had been one of the children up to the day of my arrival.

Our building was in the middle of a meadow, about 200 metres away from the main building in which lived over 100 children. Our building was really just a wooden hut, completely open in the front, and the children's beds were all in one long row. That year we had very unusual weather. After a wet April we had snow in May. Sometimes we had to shake off the snow from the children's pillows in the evening. We put the children to bed, dressed in wool sweaters, wearing wool stockings, wool caps on their heads, oil lotion on their faces and hands. And into each bed we put a hot brick wrapped up in newspaper. Sometimes I was awakened in the night by a crying child, who wanted to go to the toilet, but could not get out of bed because we had tucked in the blankets so tightly.

For their weekly warm bath we took the children up to the main house. For their daily wash we carried the water in buckets down from the main house. The meals were brought down to us from the main house kitchen. Mind you, this was the year 1929. There was a big reform in nourishment. One ate, so to say, calories. Dr Robert worked out how many calories each child should eat according to his or her age and body-weight. With every dinner I received the written information, which told me for instance: Spinach 40 calories per 100 grammes, Pudding 45 calories, and so on. And I had to weigh every child's dinner, every item of it, after calculating in my head (adding machines did not exist yet) what to serve each child. But mind you, no allowance was made for those calories which the children left on their plates by not finishing it all.

The home was open for visitors at weekends only. Dr Robert did not want any child in the Open Air Department to be sick in bed at weekends, but I refused to let a sick child get up just for the weekend. We had arguments over several things, and after six months I handed in my resignation. Dr Robert refused to accept it. I asked her: "Why?" Her answer was: "I will not let my best nurse leave." But I was determined to leave. When the day came for me to pack up my things, I could not find my suitcase. It had disappeared from my room. I searched everywhere, then I asked the gardener if he had seen it. "Look in the chicken coop", he said, and there I found it.

What had kept me in the *Sängerwarte* for so long? I liked the children. I liked the location right in the open country. With a view over the whole city! I worked with enthusiasm, six days a week from 6.00am to 9.30pm. But I refused to do things which I knew it was wrong to do.

A man in my life

Whilst I was working there at the *Sängerwarte*, it happened that my sister droppped in one evening at 9.30 with a friend of hers on her evening walk. They found me standing in front of the cottage. I was standing there in my nurse's uniform with a big apron on top of it, in one hand one of the children's shoes, and in the other a brush to polish it. Yes, I stood there in the meadows surrounded by a circle of twenty pairs of children's shoes, which I was just cleaning. At the sight of my sister, I said: "Oh, isn't it beautiful here - look at the view! You can see all over Vienna, the Prater, even the *Riesenrad* going round!" And my sister said: "I wouldn't give a damn about the view if I had to clean twenty pairs of children's shoes in the evening at 9.30."

Two days later my sister called me up and said: "The friend I was with, Hans, would like to meet you again." "OK", I said. So Hans and I met again on one of my days off in the afternoon, and we got in the habit of meeting once a week in the late afternoon for a walk in the hills surrounding Vienna. We always made sure to be back in front of the *Sängerwarte* before 10.00 o'clock in the evening, because at that time the main door of the house was locked for the night, and I wanted to be there before they locked up. We were always there, but I never went in, because it took us a long time to say good-bye to each other. We always still had something to talk about, and we were not aware that one hour slipped by after another; before we knew it, it was 5.00 o'clock in the morning. So what now? Of course I couldn't ring the front door bell in the morning at 5.00 o'clock. So I always climbed back into the garden over the high wooden fence.

Some weeks after we had met, Hans asked me to marry him, but I refused. Why? Because Hans was a professor at the University of Vienna. There was a lot of anti-Semitism in Vienna and I was convinced that he wouldn't be accepted in society if he was married to a Jew. I broke off our friendship for his sake, though I felt very bad about it as I really liked him very much.

Back to Germany

In October 1929 I went back to Berlin and opened a private nursery school. I ran that school in a very modern and progressive way; I was very proud to have children of four or five different nationalities. I had small children in the mornings, and in the afternoon a group of school children for handicrafts and so on. Twice a week I held a play afternoon where everything we did was done in the English language. The children loved that. I remember the mother of a 3-year-old came to me and said: "What's going on here in your nursery school? My little boy counts up to 20 in English, and he knows all the colours in English."

The following year I had two weeks vacation in Vienna and afterwards returned by boat to Linz, and from there by train, but when I showed my ticket at the gate, the man said: "This is no good." "Why not?" "It is not a return ticket." I had been under the impression that it was, and I had no money to buy a new ticket. "Can I pay for it in Berlin?" I asked. "No!" he said in a rough way. "What can I do?" "Stay here and get the money", he said.

The train was due in ten minutes. I bought a platform ticket, but when I showed him the platform ticket he would not let me through either.

29

"I have the right to get on the platform with this ticket", I argued. His answer was: "You want to get on the train with it. I will not let you." Then I just walked through. Two minutes later two policemen arrested me, and took me to the police station on that train station. I told them my story. To no avail. Then I said I wanted to see the train driver when the train arrived. The policemen were not in favour. They argued: "The train will only be here for three minutes. The train driver will have no time to be bothered. He will not want to see you." "I am sure that he will take me on his train. I want to speak to him", I said.

When the train drove into the station, one of the two policemen went out. He came back into the police station with the train driver. "My lady, what can I do for you?" the train driver asked me. "Take me with you to Berlin", and while I said it, I took my watch off my wrist and handed it to him. "Keep your watch, I don't need it, and come with me." Happily I walked off with the train driver. Early in the morning we got into Berlin. Two hours later I knocked on the dormitory door of the men who worked on the trains. My train driver was almost in tears when I gave him the money for my fare, and a box of cigars.

———

In the summer of 1931 I took a job at a children's vacation home at Norderney on the North Sea. I had applied by letter. They had told me that they would have 45 children and 4 adults in charge of those 45 children. When I arrived, there were 90 children, and only two adults in charge. The first morning, when after breakfast I started to clear the tables, the Director stopped me. "No, no!" she said, "Don't clear the tables. Only take a damp cloth and wipe the plates off, and leave everything on the table for the next meal."

In the home's leaflet it said that the children would have fowl for dinner twice a week. That really was a 'foul' statement. They bought four chickens for 90 children plus staff. At those chicken dinners, the Director herself would walk around the tables with a big chicken platter and ask every single child: "Would you rather have little bones or skin?" In the evening, the Director would stand at the bottom of the stairs with a candy jar, and pop a candy into every child's mouth as they went up to their dormitories. What a camp that was! I was relieved to get back to my own private nursery school.

My nursery school, which ran very well indeed, unfortunately came to an end in 1933 when Hitler came to power. Then of course I realised right away that as a Jew I wouldn't be able to conduct my school in the way I wanted to. Therefore I closed the school on 1st April and made arrangements to leave the country. I thought: 'I am really lucky because I am working with children, and there are children all over the world. Wherever I go I can find children, and I can find work with children.' I sat down and thought: 'Where shall I go to find a new livelihood?'

And then an idea came to me. I sat down and wrote twenty letters to resorts and Chambers of Commerce in Switzerland. This is how my letter started: "Do you know that in Germany there is a profession known as *Hotelkindergärtnerin*?" Actually it did not exist, but I went on to say: "There are many advantages of having such a person in your hotel. For the hotel, there is a separate children's dining room. Every morning the *Kindergärtnerin* discusses the menu to be served in the children's dining room with the head waiter. She eats with the children. After lunch the children have a rest period under the supervision of the *Kindergärtnerin*, who takes care of the children from early morning all through the day. That eliminates complaints from other guests about 'noisy children'. Financially, the *Kindergärtnerin* does not cost the hotel anything; the hotel gives her free board and a room, and the parents are charged 1% or 2% for the service of the *Kindergartnerin* on their hotel bill. Advantages for the parents: their children are well taken care of from morning to night. Advantages for the children: the company of other children, and they will all enjoy handicrafts, hiking and swimming."

While I was writing these letters, my mother came into my room. "What are you doing?" she asked. I told her, and she said: "Don't write those letters." "Why not?" Her answer was: "It is a waste of paper! A waste of time, a waste of stamps! Nobody will answer!" "Mother", I said, "If only one of those 20 letters will bring me an answer, that is all I need: only one answer." And the answer came from Engelberg, and this was the reply: "We do not have families with children until June, but if you are in Berlin at the moment, you might like to have a vacation and we invite you to be our guest throughout the month of May."

Engelberg

The ages of the children under my care in Engelberg were between 2 and 12 years, and of course I had to talk in different languages.

Fortunately I did know German, English, French and Italian, the four languages which I needed. I enjoyed that summer very much, and returned again for the next summer. That second summer there were many more children in my group. I ventured to ask some of the German mothers: "Why did you come to Engelberg?" The answer was: "Because you are here." Word had gone around that there was somebody in Engelberg to take care of the children.

One evening, a hotel guest, an invalid named Schmidt, came to me and said: "I want to marry you." "What?" I said, "You want to marry me? You don't even know me." "Yes" he said, "I have been watching you with your group of children in the open-air swimming pool for over a week. I like the way you handle them, and I want to marry you." I said: "But I don't want to marry YOU." He said: "You would be very stupid not to, because I am Swiss, and if you marry me, you won't have to go back to Germany. You become Swiss by marriage." I said:" Listen, Mr. Schmidt, that surely wouldn't be any reason for me to marry you", and I turned away from him.

Some days later, after dinner, I intended to go up the road to the Hotel Engels, the last hotel at the end of the village. As I came out, it was pouring. I stood there for a minute, and then decided to go up to my room, change, and get a raincoat and an umbrella. As I turned round, there stood Mr. Schmidt, who said: "Are you going out? In this weather? I can take you wherever you want to go." I said: "No thank you. I am all right." He said: "Where are you going?" I said: "Only up the road to the Hotel Engels. I'll be all right." But he said: "Look, my car is right in front of the hotel. I will take you. You don't have to be afraid that I might take you somewhere else. I couldn't, because the road finishes there. Let me take you."

I got in, and we drove off, but he didn't stop in front of the Hotel Engels. He went on and up into the forest. I said to him: "Look, you are on a forbidden road. You aren't allowed to drive on this road." He answered: "I'm always on forbidden roads. All my life. I don't mind", and on he went. I begged him to stop the car and let me get out, but he wouldn't. The road snaked up the side of the mountain. It was pouring with rain, and foggy, and the further we drove, the worse the weather got.

After a long time, the road became too narrow for the car. We came to a stop. He turned off the lights and said: "We'll just have to stay here for a while." "I will not", I said, opened the door, and got out. There I stood, in the pitch dark, in heavy fog, heavy rain. What should I do now? I was really scared to walk down by myself in the dark, with the rain pouring down and puddles wherever I stepped, but what else could I do? I said: "I am not staying. I am going down." Now he changed his tactics. He said: "You cannot leave me here alone, in this weather. I am an invalid. I don't have my crutches with me but I cannot walk without them. If you don't want to stay here with me, then you must take me down again. But we can't leave the car here." I said: "Look, nobody can steal the car, because nobody can drive it any further, or turn it round either." "All right", he said, "I'll go down with you."

I took off my suede shoes with high heels, and my stockings, and we started to walk. This big heavy man was at my side, his arm resting heavily on my shoulder. With every step we took, the water splashed up from the puddles, and ran down my hair and over my face. To one side the ground fell away into the valley, to the other it rose steeply up the mountain-side. One wrong step and we would have fallen and been killed. We had a long, long walk down that mountain. Finally, after some hours, we came to the end of the forest, and the outskirts of the village. "Now you have to fend for yourself", I said to him, and walked back through the village by myself. I was embarrassed to be seen walking into the hotel with him. It had truly been the worst night of my life.

For the next eight days I wasn't bothered by Mr Schmidt. He was sulking because I had left him on the outskirts of the village. Then suddenly he came to me again. This time he looked very boisterous, and said: "I will tell you something. You didn't want to marry me, and now I'm going to marry Mrs. Meyer. I don't like her, but I am going to marry her just to spite you." He married Mrs. Meyer, and some days later, I heard that he had been in a bad car accident; both of them were killed on the spot. I did come back to Engelberg again for the following summer, but further adventures were waiting for me in England in the meantime.

Off to London

I had met a German family from Nürnberg at the end of my first summer in Engelberg who needed a governess to go with them to London, and I accepted the job. I made one condition: I told the lady that I would stay with her only two months, to help her get settled, because she didn't know any English at all. My English wasn't good either, but at least I could make myself understood. After two months, I told her: "You must take an English governess so the children can learn English, and I will go to an English family."

By that time winter had come; it was very cold and foggy in London, and I took jobs in private houses as governess or nurse. As a nurse in a high-class English family, I was completely isolated; I didn't belong to the family as I was only the nurse, but I wasn't allowed to communicate with the kitchen staff or the maids either. I didn't eat at the table with the family, but neither did I eat in the kitchen with the cook and the chambermaid. My meals were brought to me on a tray into my bedroom.

That was my winter of 1933/34. I found that in England at that time the ideas on how to treat pre-school children were very traditional. Five-year-olds were still taken out in big prams, and when there was a younger child in the family I had to use the so-called double-pram. I was in one family where there was a child of 2 and one of 5. I had to wheel those two children in the pram to St James' Park with a tricycle and a football on top of the pram. Arriving in the park, the children were allowed to run around and play. After two hours the children were lifted back onto the pram and the heavy thing was pushed back home.

In one house where I nursed there was a 3-year old boy. The parents told me to take him to Hyde Park in his pram, and there I was to sit on a certain bench with the child in the pram. Half an hour later the parents came riding up on horses. Each of the parents was on one horse, and between them was a third horse, for the child. The child was lifted out of the pram and on to the horse. While he went riding with his parents, I sat in the park watching the empty pram, and after an hour the parents brought the child back. He was lifted off the horse and back into the pram; his feet never touched the ground. Five-year-old children were taken to school in their prams. In front of the school, the child would be given his bag to put on his back and sent up to school, and at 12.00 o'clock you could see all the prams and nannies standing in front of the school, waiting for their charges.

———

At the end of that winter I found a furnished room in a terraced house. It was a pretty large room on the top floor. The first night in that room I had retired early to get a good night's sleep. As soon as I turned off the light, they started their game: mice — a whole lot of them. They threw over the waste paper basket. They were here and there and everywhere. I turned on the light, and saw them disappear in all directions, but as soon as I turned off the light again, they were back. They kept me up all night. In the morning I complained to the landlady. "Do not feel so bad about it", said Mrs Taylor, "There are mice in every room." "I do not want to share my room with mice", I told her. "Well", she said, "I can give you a mousetrap." "No! Oh no! I will not have a mousetrap in my room, and find an injured or dead mouse in the trap!" "Then, Miss Karger, there is nothing I can do. It is your own problem."

It was a problem. How could I get rid of those mice without hurting them? I went and bought a piece of cake. That evening I broke it up in little bits, put it on a saucer out in the hall, outside my door, with the waste paper basket in the door to keep it open. I hoped that the mice would just use my room as a passageway to get to the cake. And it seemed to work. That night I did not hear the mice, and in the morning the saucer was empty. So again I bought cake for the nightly dinner of the mice, and again I found the saucer empty in the morning. For a third time I provided their dinner. But that third morning Mrs Taylor came up to see me. "Miss Karger", she said, "Now I have a complaint. You are feeding the mice out in the hall. They are going out of your room and into all the other rooms. You cannot do that. Everybody has to keep their own mice."

Solving a financial problem

As the weeks went past, I felt I had to solve my money problem. A gas meter had to be fed with pennies to provide heat; another meter to provide hot water; a third to provide light, and I was short on pennies, very short. So I put a little advertisement in the daily paper: 'Lady wants to share her flat'. I received a phone call: "Are you the lady who wants to share the flat?" "Yes, I am." "May I ask you some questions?" "Go ahead." "Would I have a bedroom?" "Oh yes, you would." "Maybe you could tell me what furniture is in the room. That would give me an idea of the size of the room." "Now let's see. There is a bed, there is a wardrobe, there is a dressing table, there is a chest of drawers, there is a card table, there is a sewing table, there is a dining table." I did not tell her that it was always the same table, which served for all the different purposes. My lodger wanted to move in the same evening. As I had to go out that evening I told her that I would leave the house key in front of the door under the mat, and the key to the flat under the mat of the door to the flat. Only she should be sure to put the keys under the mats again, otherwise she would lock me out since I would be home very late.

After our conversation on the phone I got busy fixing up my lodger's 'room'. With a piece of white chalk I divided the room into two. I even drew a connecting door. I moved my bedding on to the couch, which was in my 'new room', put clean sheets on her bed. On her pillow I put an apple with a note: 'I wish you a good night. I am looking forward to seeing you tomorrow morning.'

On my way home, late at night, I wondered: 'Will she have come? Will she have remembered to put the keys back under the mats?' I found my house door key under the mat. I walked up the four flights. 'Oh yes, there is the key. Will she be there?' Carefully I opened the door. Someone was lying in the bed, but I could not see her. She had the blankets pulled over her head. I did not wake her up. I got undressed in the hall, just with my small torch, and tiptoed to my couch. There I found an orange on my pillow with a note: 'Thank you for the apple. That was very sweet of you. I wish you a good night. I will see you tomorrow morning.'

That night I did not sleep much. It was a funny feeling to have some-one sleep in the same room whom you had never seen before. In the morning I waited and waited for her to wake up. Finally she did wake up. She sat up in her bed. I sat up in mine. We stared at each other. No one spoke. Then after a couple of minutes we both burst out laughing. She was tall and blonde with big blue eyes. I was small with dark hair and black eyes. I said: "Now we are going to play a game." "What game?" she asked. I explained: "Today, I am the lady and you are the maid. You must go down to buy fresh rolls and a newspaper and then make break-fast and serve it to me. Tomorrow you will be the lady and I will be the maid."

We became good friends. We lived together in poverty for about two months, and enjoyed it. Every Monday we put a certain amount of money, which had to last us for that week, in our purse, and that was it. And we did manage. For instance, on Monday we put three pennies into the meter and enjoyed a full hot bath. On Tuesday we had twopence worth of hot water, on Wednesday only one penny worth. If our purse was empty on Sunday, we would stay in bed all day. Then we told ourselves: in bed you do not get dirty; you do not need a bath. In bed you do not need light. You do not need to heat the room. You do not need food. Just rest and sleep. Sometimes we already had to resort to our beds on Saturday.

The morning after Mary had moved in I thought I must tell my land-lady. Down I went to her flat. "Mrs. Taylor, I have good news for you!" "What is the good news?" she asked. "Mrs. Taylor, up to now I have paid you ten shillings a week. From now on I will pay you twelve." "How come?" "Mrs. Taylor, I took in a friend of mine as a guest for a little while. It's only fair, I think, to pay you a little more." Mrs. Taylor was very pleased. So were Mary and I who shared the rent between us.

Mary, the daughter of a publisher, had come to England to better her English. She had taken a job as cook in a private family. What she learnt was that she had not improved her English. The pots and pans had not spoken to her. As my English was also very poor we, the German and the Norwegian, spoke French with each other in England.

Another man in my life

In the spring of 1934 another man entered my life whom I met while in the Lyons Corner House at Marble Arch with a friend. We were both too poor to order a proper meal but he had just ordered a big pancake, and I wondered out loud if he could share it with us. No sooner had I said it, when he got up and came over to our table. "Excuse me", he said, "but I heard you talk in German. May I join you?"

He went and got his pancake. What a beautiful pancake. How I longed to taste it. It smelled delicious. And here I was, sitting with my pot of tea and my two hot cross buns. That had been my nourishment for a week: once a day, a pot of tea and two hot cross buns. It was all that I could afford. I had told myself: 'ONE person needs only ONE meal a day. And for variety's sake I will do it this way. One day I will have it at breakfast time, one day at lunch time and one day at dinner time.' In between these, my meals, I smoked some cigarettes, which covered up, or chased away, the feeling of being hungry.

I used to take these 'meals' in the brasserie of the Lyons Corner House at Marble Arch. I liked the atmosphere there: the musicians in their Tyrolean leather trousers, white shirts and embroidered braces, and their accordions. Dr. Charles, who had joined us at our table with his pancake, had come to London from Budapest on business. He and I became good friends, and we spent many happy hours together. I had appreciated Charlie's honesty very much. He had told me at our first meeting that he was married and had a wife at home in Budapest. He himself was sent by his firm to London for six months to start a new factory, and, as he told me, he was very lonely for his wife and I reminded him of her. She too was short, had black hair and black eyes. She was also very lively, as I was, and that was what had attracted him to me.

Knowing that Charlie was married, I thought that nothing could happen between us. It would just be a nice loose friendship. But soon I fell deeply in love him, and then I made him move from his hotel to my guest-house. Each of us had our own room, I on the top floor, he on the ground floor, but we visited each other. He spent most of the night in my room, then in the early morning at 5.00 o'clock he would go down to his own room, but an hour later I couldn't be without him any more, and I went down to his room. Then at 7.00 o'clock I would go to the kitchen and tell them: "Dr Charles is having his breakfast with me. Please bring it up for us here." At 8.00 o'clock he would be off to the factory, and an hour later he would call me up to hear how I was. At 5.00 o'clock he would be back, then we would go out to have dinner together. We really lived together, but we never had intercourse, because whenever he wanted to, I said: "No, you have a loving wife at home and I respect her rights. I would never do that to another woman - to cheat her." So, as I said, we lived together for three happy weeks.

Then he went home for ten days, and promised to call me up as soon as he was back from Budapest. When the ten days were up I called the factory where he was a director and asked him if he had brought back any news from Budapest. "Yes", he said. "What is the news?" "I brought my wife. My wife is back here with me. And now", he said, "Ilse, we can only meet all three of us together. I cannot see you any more alone." That was of course a shock to me. He said: "I will tell my wife that I met you at a mutual friend's house, and I think we ought to invite you over sometimes." So he now lived in a hotel again, away from me, and he told me to befriend his wife and to help her because she didn't know any English. I should help her get around in London while he was busy in the factory and try to spend quite a lot of time with her. That's what I did, and to the outside world she and I became friends, but it was very difficult for me to visit them for dinner or go out with them. There was this deep friendship between him and me, and we had to try to ignore it in the presence of his wife. I think his wife sensed it, but she was a very nice and a very good person, and so we three managed for a while to make a go of it. But it was very painful for me - very painful.

Berlin - the final chapter

In Autumn 1934 I went back to Germany to prepare my emigration to America. Of course my father didn't want me to go. He said: "Don't go to America." "Why not?" I said. "Only criminals go to America. If you go to America, our relatives and friends would think that you have to leave Germany because you have broken the law. You cannot go to America, and since I don't want you to go, I won't give you any financial help to get there, and as you yourself don't have enough money, you just won't go. That's how it is." "Father", I said, "I can understand your point of view, but I am determined to go. I will find a way to get there without money, but it will take me longer, that's all." That was in October 1934. In January 1935 I left Germany for America, and the trip didn't cost me a penny. How was that?

One needed an affidavit to get in. I had an uncle in America, my mother's brother, who had emigrated from Vienna in 1894 because he had met anti-semitism in Vienna as a young doctor, and in America he had become a well-known eye surgeon. I asked him for an affidavit. He was already over 70, and wrote back: "First of all you have to tell me how you intend to make a living in America." I wrote back to him: "I am a trained nursery school teacher, group worker, nurse for sick infants and children. I am sure that in one of those professions I will be able to take care of myself. All I ask is that you help me get into the country."

My uncle gave me the affidavit. I went to the Jewish community in Berlin and said: "I am going to America. I have an affidavit. I have a passport. Do you send any groups of Jewish children to America to get them to safety?" They said: "How many would you take?" "Twenty-five. I am used to working with groups of children". A week later they gave me a departure date.

22/1/93

ℓΥΛ

40

CHAPTER 3

AMERICA

Off to America

I LEFT BERLIN on the 29th January 1935. I was on my way to a new beginning. The parting from my parents was not easy. "Where will you be? How will you make your living?" These questions were asked and could not be answered. The train took me from Berlin to Hamburg where I was to pick up 25 children. These children were strangers to me, also strangers to each other. They came from all over Germany; their families were sending them out of Germany for their own and the children's safety, hoping to be able to join up with them again. The Nazis had begun to bribe schoolchildren, giving them a reward for informing them whether their parents spoke against Hitler. The children would get a chocolate bar, while their parents would be taken away to be shot. Later, when conditions got worse, Jewish children were not even allowed to attend state schools.

In Hamburg I met the children for the first time. It was in a large room. At one end the children were standing in one long row. At the opposite end I was asked to sit down. The children were told: "That is the lady who will take you to New York - now one after the other take two steps forward, bow or curtsey and say your name." Then I was told: "Come to the boat at 6.00 pm." At the appointed time I got on the boat. In one of the lounges I found the children and their relatives: parents, grandparents, uncles and aunts. The parents were all crying. It was like a mass funeral. When the first whistle blew the Captain asked me to tell the parents to leave the boat.

"That is not my job", I said, "You are in charge of this boat, not I." "I know", said the Captain, "Yes, I know, but you as a woman will do it better, gentler and kinder." I tried to pull myself together. I said: "May I please have everybody's attention. The boat is leaving now. When it is starting to move it might be rocking badly. It's easier for you children to get into your beds before that happens. Go to your cabins now and go to bed. Your parents can visit you when you are in bed."

The children ran off, everyone eager to be the first in bed, and now I had a chance to talk to the parents. "I know how you feel", I said, "I left my old parents in Berlin this morning. I do not know if I will ever see them again. But your children are young. For them to go to America is an adventure. Try not to make it too hard for them. Go down to their cabins, say good night to them. When the children get up tomorrow morning they will be well on their way. They will have a lot to see and enjoy."

When the second whistle blew I went from cabin to cabin and asked the parents to leave. They left - but a minute later they went back in again of course - then the third whistle blew, the final one. Now I told the parents: "If you do not want to travel with us to Cherbourg you must get off in a hurry." I saw them walk away. I still see them, those poor parents.

Now I had to be on the job. It was a full-time job, twenty-five children day and night. That first evening the head waiter of the kosher kitchen approached me. He wanted to know whether we were going to eat kosher food. "I will tell you tomorrow morning", I said. The next morning I assembled the children in the lounge. "Which of you does not eat kosher food at home? Put up your hand please." Twenty hands went up. Five children came from Orthodox families. I said: "All right, we will all eat kosher meals." "Why?" some of the children said, "Why?" "Because we are one group. The children from Orthodox families are not allowed to eat non-kosher. And it does not hurt us to eat kosher for 12 days. And now listen, children. Do not storm into the dining room. Yesterday you all ran in to find the best seat. So today walk in quietly to that same place which you had yesterday."

We sat at five separate tables. They could not be moved together. They were screwed to the floor. I had appointed one child at each table to act as head of that table. After the first day, the mealtimes went off very smoothly. I had invited some of the children - the very lively ones - to join my table where I could control them. The Chef of the kosher kitchen was so happy that we ate kosher, that he treated us royally. We got the food which was served to the first-class passengers, though we travelled in third-class.

It was the worst time of the year to cross the Channel. We were not even in the North Sea but still on the River Elbe when the first child was seasick. This was my first trip on an ocean liner and when that first child was seasick I asked the Steward for a bucket and a rag. "What for?" he said. "One of my children was sick, I want to clean it up." "You don't do that", he said, "We take care of that." And when we passed the coast of Ireland most passengers were seasick. Of my twenty-five children - how many? All twenty-five. But I was not sick. I did not have time to be sea-sick.

I asked the Deck Steward for some deckchairs. He informed me that each chair cost $1 and each blanket $1. But all I had in my possession was $3. That was all the German Government had allowed me, a Jew, to take out of the country. So what could I do? I went to the Captain and explained to him that I needed at least three or four deckchairs, so the children could take turns to lie down. I told him that it would help the Stewards if the children could be kept on deck in fresh air and would not dirty the cabins. He gave me three deckchairs and blankets, but made me sign a paper that those $6 would be paid in New York before I left the boat.

In general the children behaved very well. Did I say in general? That is right. One day, while we were all on deck, I thought: 'Where is Robert?' He was one of the big boys, 13. We started to look for him - it became almost a treasure hunt. We walked through the second-class deck and social rooms, through the first-class, then up to the bridge guided by one of the Stewards. Finally we found Robert. Where? In the engine room. And then I made an agreement with Robert. He always told me: "I'm going down to visit - you know where!" Yes, I knew where. Then there was Peter, about 10 years old. He leaned over the railing on deck one day - he was hanging over with half of his body. I pulled him back. I sent him down to his cabin in my anger. Later I went down to talk to him. The poor kid explained: "I was feeling sick, and I did not want to do it on the floor."

I did not get much sleep in those twelve nights. I had the children in eight or nine cabins. I checked on everybody several times a night. Once two boys came to me in the middle of the night. They wanted to go on deck because the German boat, S.S. Bremen, was passing us, and if I would not go with them they would go without me. I went with them.

I tried to keep the children busy and happy. I also gave them an English lesson every day. In Cherbourg, our first and only stop, we went ashore and took a good long hike for two hours. How happy the children were to know that they had been in France.

When after 12 days we approached New York, the Immigration Officers came on board. I presented my own and the children's passports. That officer asked me: "Have you $36 landing money?" "No, I don't." "Didn't you know that you must have that?" "Yes, I did, but the Germans did not allow me to take more than $3. I have only $3." "Sorry, but I cannot let you get off the boat." "Sir", I said, "could you tell me where on my way I could have fished for those $36 in the ocean?" He changed the subject.

We got in to the harbour. It was bitterly cold. All first-class passengers got off the boat, then second-class, then third-class and we as refugees last. Then we had to stand in a kind of open shelter, up to our ankles in the snow, and I had to open all the children's trunks and my own for inspection. Finally we were all loaded on to an open van and driven through New York to the Clara de Hirsch Home where the children were to stay until private families were found to take them in as foster children.

The Home was a Jewish foundation, a residence for young girls and young women in New York aged 18 - 30 who were not earning more than $25 per week. The home provided basic single rooms, breakfast and dinner. I was given hospitality for the first night, and the next day I was invited to stay on. I was offered a room and free board in exchange for taking care of the children.

Some of the boys, all healthy and full of energy, were quite mischievous. Once, in the middle of the night, I was awakened by the siren of fire engines. I looked out of the window. They were parking in front of our building. The firemen came dashing in to look for the fire — but there was no fire. Kind neighbours had given the alarm when they saw two of our boys climb down the fire escape outside the building, from the third floor, clad in their pyjamas. Another difficulty was the 'schooling' of these children. They were sent to the local primary school. There they were, sitting in the same class-room with American six-year-olds. Of course they felt bored and humiliated, those boys of 10 to 14 years of age, and they became impossible. After some days they were thrown out of the school.

About two weeks later I got my first taste of a demonstration. Two young girls, residents of Clara de Hirsch Home, approached me with a petition sheet. "Please sign this", they said. "We need your signature."

"What is it for?" I asked. "You don't have to read it. Just sign." I did not sign. The next day, the 'demonstration' took place: about 50 people, men and women of all ages. About 10 of them were our residents. They carried large placards. They walked around our whole block. They shouted: "We want better food and lower rates." Stones were hurled at our building, windows broken. Our director asked for police protection. For two days a policeman was stationed in our entrance hall; the front door was kept locked.

After the demonstration, those residents who had been in it were told by the police officer: "You do not live here any more; here is your new address. Your private belongings are also at your new hotel. Your rent for your first week is also paid." The weekly rent there was of course much higher than it was in Clara de Hirsch Home; the girls begged to be allowed back, but were not taken in.

―――

My first summer in the USA found me in Camp Lenore, a privately owned girls camp for children of well-off families. I was employed as 'Housemother' of the junior camp. This meant that I was a housekeeper and supervisor for the physical care of 30 children, who lived in small cottages; each cottage had five children and one young counsellor. The cottages consisted of just one room, containing six beds; under each bed the camp trunk belonging to the person who occupied the bed. Adjoining this room was a toilet. Behind the cottage a clothes line. A very small hand-basin was fixed in one corner. I lived in one of those cottages with the five youngest children. We all wore camp uniform, children and adults alike: green cotton shorts, white shirts and green silk ties.

During the first week, the director told me: "I hate your German cleanliness and tidiness. I have been running this camp for 20 years. No one has ever yet asked for buckets." But at the end of that summer, the director asked me to come back again the next summer. And I did go back, and I found it a little easier. Now the children did hang their wet towels and bathing suits on the line behind the cottage, and did not throw them into their trunks on top of their clean laundry. Why had I asked for a bucket for each cottage? I did not want five children to brush their teeth and spit into that tiny hand-basin in which they all washed their faces and hands. Also for time-saving: now one child could brush her teeth over the bucket while another one used the washbasin, and they did not have to fight for the basin.

During this second year the nurse left suddenly, and I was asked to replace her and run the infirmary. I liked that job. But again, a small problem arose. Some of the smaller children paid me visits when they were supposed to be somewhere else. For instance, Jane would come and would say: "I have a cut on my finger; you cannot see it, but it's really there. Can I stay here with you?" Then a new rule was made by the director: every child who came to me should have a note from her counsellor, that she had been sent to see me. I was also told that I made it too pleasant for the sick children, but the doctor was on my side. We thought that it was right to keep the children who had to be confined to the infirmary as contented and cheerful as possible. That doctor and I became good friends.

I will never forget my first Christmas Eve in New York. I lived in a small furnished room. I ate - whenever I had some money - in cheap little corner coffee shops; a plate of soup and a sandwich. That first Christmas Eve I felt lonely and sad, so I walked down the five flights of stairs from my little room. I wanted to see people in the streets, and window displays and lighted Christmas trees. I took a walk down Fifth Avenue, the heart of the city. But that 'Heart of the City' seemed cold and dead. It was only 7.00 pm, but the street seemed deserted. There was no one about. The stores were closed and the shades in the windows drawn down.

There was nothing to see. I was all alone. In a city of 80,000 people. On Christmas Eve! Yes, everybody was at home with their own family. Didn't I have a family? Didn't I have a home? No, I had no home. My home in Germany had been taken away from me, and America was not yet my home. I was allowed to be there, but I was not really accepted. I was regarded as a 'refugee'. There were hard stones, the pavement, under my feet, and high dark buildings on each side of me, and a little bit of grey sky above me. A cold wind swept me almost off my feet. Miserable and cold, I went back to my little furnished room.

I had registered with a nursing agency. I was 'on call' now to be sent on a nursing job. But it was not easy to get such a job. I was waiting already two weeks to be 'called'. And while I was waiting my savings melted away and the day came when I had only 5 cents left. And on that very same day I received a post card from my aunt: "Call me up as soon as you receive this card."

46

With my last nickel I called up my aunt. I thought: "Maybe she will invite me for dinner." Yes, she did invite me - for next Saturday. But there were five days between now and Saturday! We chatted on the phone for a little while. Then I heard my nickel drop. So I said, "Goodbye now." And then I faced my empty purse. Also my stomach felt empty. I tried to console myself. I told myself: "I am really lucky. Things can't get any worse. Things can only get better. Now I know where I am standing, and I don't have to try to decide how best to use my last nickel." And I thought of the old German saying: "*Wenn die Not am Größten ist, ist Gottes Hilfe am nächsten*" (When the need is greatest, God's help is nearest).

But I was very hungry! What could I do? I opened my wardrobe. I looked around in it. I picked up my good shoes. I took them to a second-hand shop to sell them. But when I got to that shop, I did not seem able to make myself walk in. I went back and forth in front of the store for quite a while. I had to give myself a real push. Finally, I opened the door. It was a long, narrow store, with the counter at the very end and an old man behind it. The man asked: "How much do you want?" "50 cents", I said. "I will give you 20", he said. "That's alright", I said. I took my 20 cents and hurried out of the store. I felt terrible — as if I had committed a crime.

Then I went to Woolworth, sat down at the counter and had the most delicious meal for my 20 cents - yellow split pea soup and a grilled cheese sandwich. I had just returned home when the long-expected call came. The agency had a 'case' for me; a sick child whose mother was a teacher. I was to be in her house the next morning at 9.00 am. I was told how to get there. It would take me well over an hour on the underground train and then a bus-ride, or a long walk.

It was good to have a job for the next day. But how would I get there? I had no money for the fare. That worried me all night. I had my suitcase packed, a white uniform, white stockings and shoes, my nurse's cap, etc. But I had no money. I braced myself, and went down stairs. As I passed the reception desk, I stopped and said to the secretary: "I wonder if you could help me out with 5 cents as I have no small change for the underground." The secretary gave me 5 cents and I was on my way.

I got on the train. It seemed a long ride and finally the train driver called out: "Last stop!" I walked up the stairs and out of the station - and found myself at the beach. I had taken a train in the wrong direction, and my nickel was gone. What now? I went back into the station. I went to

47

the ticket counter. I explained where I wanted to go, that I had made a mistake. "What can I do now?" I asked. "You just have to go back where you came from", was the answer. "How can I get to the platform?" "Put a nickel in." "Where?" "Into the slot at the turnstile."

I could not bring myself to tell him that I hadn't got a nickel. I walked up to the turnstile, I looked at the slot. I said: "How do you do it?" The man called out to me: "Don't you see that slot? Just put your money in there." And again I said: "How do you do it?" Now he came out of his booth to help me. "Give me your money, I will put it in for you." I showed him my empty hand. "Pick up the chain and walk through." I refused to do that. Now he opened the chain and made me go through.

It took me over two hours to reach my destination, the house of the teacher. I was very worried. 'Would she still want me? Or would she have taken someone else because I did not come?' Well, she greeted me in a very friendly way and seemed glad that I had come. She briefed me on the patient, introduced me to the kitchen and was gone. At 5.30 she was back home again and very pleased to find a contented, happy child and a cooked dinner waiting for her. "You may go home now, I can manage. I will expect you tomorrow morning at 9.00 am", she said. I went to change into my street clothes. But how would I, how could I, get home? I had no money for the underground fare. It was much too far to walk. Well, when I was dressed and ready to leave I opened door to the living room once more and said: "I am on my way now. Goodbye Richie, good-bye Mrs Turner." "Wait a minute, Miss Karger. Do you want to be paid at the end of the week or would you like to be paid each day?" said Mrs Turner. Lucky me! Now I had money. Money for the fare, money for my meals. And I did not have to ask for it. It was given to me. It was like a present from heaven.

Meeting my parents again

On that drab winter morning in January 1935 when I left Berlin to emigrate to the USA as a German Jew, my father, who was 70, said to me: "You will not see me again, I am too old to resettle. What would I do in New York? I don't speak English. Here I have my business." And he added: "I want to be buried in Weissensee, where my parents are buried." And when I said goodbye to mother she said: "You will never see me again. I cannot come to America, I get seasick on a boat." "Mother", I said, "I will visit you next year. We can meet in Switzerland or in Italy for your 60th birthday."

48

I knew that I would not have American citizenship until five years had passed. I also knew that my German passport was valid for only one more year. Then I would be without any passport for four years. So it was that after a year in New York I was facing this problem: the promise to my mother. But I had no money to buy a ticket. I found out that the fare could be paid with German money in Germany, provided I travelled on a German liner and the ticket was a gift from a relative. I acted on that.

I sent a telegram to my father: 'Please pay 500 Marks to Nord Deutscher Lloyd. Cabin already reserved for 29.IV.' Two days later I received a telegram from my father: 'ALLES NACH WUNSCH ERLEDIGT' - everything done according to your wishes. The next step was to get a visa from the German Consul. The German Consul told me in confidence not to visit Germany any more. "I won't", I said. "For financial reasons I will travel on the S.S.Bremen, but I will leave her in Cherbourg. I have taken an all-through concession ticket to Venice."

Conditions in Berlin had got much worse and my parents felt now that they could or should not leave the house together, not both at the same time. Therefore I was to have a holiday with father in Switzerland first, and then with mother. In Paris, at the main post office, I would find a letter telling me where I would meet father. I travelled to Paris. I went to the main post office. I got father's letter. He wrote that he could not leave home because Happy (the dog) was sick with indigestion, and he wanted to supervise Happy's diet, but mother would meet me in Venice.

There was also a letter from mother. She wrote: 'I expect to arrive in Venice on Thursday. If the Hotel Bel Sole where father and I spent our honeymoon 36 years ago still exists, I will be there, otherwise you will find a letter in the main post office.'

After reading mother's letter I thought, 'I want to be in Venice when she arrives, I want to greet her right at the station'. This was already Wednesday noon. I left Paris the same evening, travelled all night, and arrived in Venice on Thursday morning. I went to look for that Hotel Bel Sole. It was still there. I checked in, then with a big bunch of flowers went back to the station. The first direct train from Berlin at 10.00 am. did not bring mother. But there was a second direct train from Berlin at 2.00 pm.

As the train rolled into the station I spotted mother. As she stepped down from the train I took her arm, to help her. "Thank you", she said.

Then, lifting up her head, she saw that it was me - and she said: "It's awful - and I don't like it! I have come only from Berlin. You have come all the way from New York, and still you have managed to be here first."

————

I returned to America after this brief reunion, but my health continued to bother me. I had to go to hospital when pleurisy was diagnosed, and after I was discharged, my doctor advised me to go to Florida for the rest of the winter. "But don't do any nursing", he said, "Take an outdoor job, any kind of outdoor job, and don't come back till the winter is over." As I was very short of money I went by coach, a twenty-four hour ride. In Miami I checked in to a cheap hotel. The next morning I went to the Employment Office and told the lady behind the window that I was looking for an outdoor job. She: "What is your profession?" I: "I don't want to do that now." She: "What is your profession?" I: "I want an outdoor job." She: "The only thing we would have to offer would be grading tomatoes." I: "Yes, that would do." She: "But it pays very little." I: "That's alright." She: "But it's not here in the city. You would have to get out there by bus early in the morning to start work at 7.00 am." I: "I would not mind."

She gave me some forms to be filled in and pointed out that every question had to be answered. These included questions such as: What is your religion, your citizenship, your school education, your acquired degrees, your professional training? How many languages do you know? Do you know them fairly well, well, or very well? Do you write them well or very well? Give your last six employers as references. What are your hobbies? The questionnaire also wanted to know all about my parents, where they lived, what they did and so on. When I brought the completed forms back, I was informed that the person who would have to see me would not be there until the afternoon, so I returned later. I was ushered into the office of the 'Director of Outdoor Jobs'. He had my application form in front of him and seemed to study it. Then he handed it back to me and said: "I am sorry Miss Karger, but you are not experienced enough."

A winter vacation

In December 1936, a previous employer asked me to take Betty on vacation for a week while she was getting married again. Betty was to

50

take her sledge along, and her mother furnished me with her skis, though I had never been on skis before. To my big surprise, our guest-house was really a riding school, and our host was the riding instructor. I had never been on a horse, but seeing the horses, that was a big temptation. 'I wish that I could try it', I thought, 'I would love to sit on a horse.'

The next morning I talked to our host. "How are you at skiing?" he asked. "I have never yet had skis under my feet", I had to admit. "Well", he said, "Take your skis and come with me." He drove me to a pretty steep hill. "Try to ski down this hill", he said. "When you are able to do that, <u>then</u> I will let you get on a horse. Now stand right here. Give yourself a good push with your sticks, throw the sticks away — and off you go."

Well, it was very hard to keep my balance. Every time I was about to fall, I just jumped out of my skis, and let the skis glide down to the bottom without me. I practised that for almost three hours, and by then I had learned to stay on my skis all the way down.

The next morning I had my first riding lesson. I was allowed to mount the horse, and the horse was led around the courtyard. The following day I was allowed in the ring, but it seemed to me that my horse and I did not speak the same language. I addressed the horse in English: "Please don't run so fast. Please stop." But he did not understand me. He galloped happily around the ring. The next day, again in the ring, I learnt to control the horse by the reins, and the next day I was taken out

together with two other riders. It was a beautiful clear winter morning. The frost glistened on the branches of the fir trees. The sun was shining; the air was crisp. I felt free and happy. It was an experience. Our bridle path took us through a lovely forest, uphill and downhill. We rode one behind the other in single file - I was the first - and it happened that my horse stumbled and went down on his front legs. I tried to stay on his back, while he tried to get back on his feet. I fell off, and he galloped away. The riding instructor brought him back soon. I managed to climb on a wooden fence, and from there back on to my horse, and we continued our lovely outing. This beautiful vacation week passed much too fast for me. It seemed to gallop away.

———

In 1937 I met Walter and his two children. We were both employed in Trudel Frankel's Home for Children, he as a Group Worker doing handicrafts with the children and I as a nurse. He had come from Vienna, and he told me that his wife had sent their children to America with a Children's Transport to get them out; after they were safe she herself went to Israel to follow another man whom she was going to marry there. She had later divorced Walter.

By 1942 our friendship had grown, and I was sharing a flat with Walter and his teenage children. One day he came home from work in the factory feeling sick, but the next day he dragged himself to work again as he insisted he couldn't afford to stay home because he was paid by the hour. The same happened on the following day. He dragged himself to work in the morning and came home half-dead on Friday evening. On Saturday he wasn't well enough to get up in the morning. He just stayed in bed. He looked very poorly to me but still he wouldn't let me call the doctor. He said: "If the doctor comes, he will put me into the hospital and that means that over the week-end I will be in the hospital and not be able to go to work on Monday. I cannot afford not to work on Monday because I need the money badly."

On Saturday afternoon he didn't seem any better and without telling him, I called the doctor. That evening at 11.00 o'clock the doctor came to pay a house visit. He walked into Walter's room to examine him and not even two minutes later he came out of the room. "Where is the nearest telephone?" he said. I heard him ask for an emergency bed and I heard him say: "Have the Operating Room ready. This is an emergency operation. I will notify the surgeon myself." Then the doctor told me to get

Walter into a taxi and take him right to the emergency hospital ward where the surgeon and he would meet me.

We arrived at the hospital - emergency admission - and I admitted Walter. When I was asked: "Who is the next-of-kin? We need the next-of-kin's signature for the operation", I said: "I am the next-of-kin", and I signed as his wife. Some minutes later the surgeon came. I was introduced to him and the surgeon asked: "Now, how long has he been sick?" When I told him four days, the surgeon said: "No, I cannot operate on him. It is too late. It's a burst appendix, and it's too late." I said to the surgeon: "If it is too late, then we cannot lose anything, we can only win. Please operate on him. He has two children who are without a mother and who need him." "OK", said the surgeon, "I will try my best. Stay in the waiting room. I will let you know." The son and I sat in the waiting room all night, that meant six long hours, anxiously waiting for the outcome of the operation.

At 5.00 o'clock in the morning the surgeon came to the waiting-room. "He is still alive", he said, "But we will not know the outcome for about ten days." Yes, ten days we had to wait anxiously for the outcome of this operation. The next day, after I came home from my factory work, I went to the hospital. I got into the elevator and said: "Fifth floor, please." The man in the elevator said: "Are you visiting a patient?" I said "Yes." "Sorry", said the man, "Visiting hour is over. I cannot take you up. I must take you down again. Come tomorrow at visiting time." He took me down to the ground floor again. I looked for the stairs and I hurried up five flights to Walter's room. All I wanted to do was to have one look at him, and this I did for the next week. Every night I went home after working in the factory all day, gave the children their supper, and then went off to the hospital where I walked up the five flights to visit Walter for some minutes.

Walter did recover fully, and some months later the estranged wife came over from Israel. She lived with us for some months as our guest and then the family looked for a better, private, flat. They found a flat, and Walter wanted me to move with them into their new flat. "No", I said, "No, Walter, you cannot live with two women in one flat." He said: "Why not? I can have my room in the middle. My wife can have her room on the right side of my room and you on the other side of my room." "No", I said, "Walter, no. That we cannot do." And so I had to give up the friendship with Walter. It was very painful for me.

———

53

In the Autumn of 1937 I knew that it was important for me to get away from the bad winter weather of New York. I had heard that Colorado had a very good climate, and thought I would be able to find a job in Denver. Of course the cheapest way was by coach, a 90-hour direct ride from New York due to leave at midnight. I joined the queue at 11.00 pm, intending to take a seat at the very back of the bus. 'If I'm lucky', I thought, 'I can stretch out over three seats and go to sleep.'

My turn came to board the coach. I had my heart set on that back seat, but a little boy was sitting right behind the driver's seat with his hand pointing to the empty seat beside him. He looked at me and said: "This seat isn't taken." He obviously wanted me to sit there, and I couldn't disappoint him. I sat down next to Johnny, and for the next four days we belonged to each other. He was 10, and his father, standing outside the coach, was giving him last minute instructions. "Don't you worry, son, your mother will be there to meet you. And don't forget to do some homework every day — your book is in the bag. And go easy on the money. Buy yourself a glass of milk and a chocolate bar every day, and if you run out of money, eat the cheese sandwiches in your bag."

The driver got into his seat, the father waved a last goodbye, and we were on our way. Johnny assured me that we were lucky: "We have the best seats", he said, "Right behind the driver; we can see everything." Johnny's luggage consisted of a paper shopping bag containing his pyjamas, a toothbrush, six handkerchiefs, six cheese sandwiches and his school book. In his pocket was his money, 40 cents — 10 for each day.

At 5.00 am we had our first stop. Our driver announced: "This is our breakfast stop. The Ladies Room is to the right, the cafetaria to the left. Please board the coach again in 25 minutes." Of course I took Johnny with me for this and every other meal. After two days Johnny was also invited for a meal by some of the other passengers. The atmosphere on these buses was always very good, friendly and cheerful. The drivers were excellent, efficient, courteous and helpful. They worked six or eight-hour shifts, and at the end of their shift they would hand over the coach and the care of the passengers to the next driver with some small remark, for instance: "Keep an eye on this young girl; she's lost her handbag once already."

We were well on our way after the breakfast break when one of the passengers, the young girl in fact, started to cry. "I've lost my handbag!" "Look on top of your seat; under your seat; on the floor", advised the

54

driver. "It's not there", she wailed, "Maybe I left it in the cafetaria." The driver made a U-turn and went back to the cafetaria. There it was.

Another of the passengers had a canary with him, which suddenly escaped from its cage. It flew around, perching on the heads of various passengers, but the owner was unable to catch it. Finally the driver stopped the bus and caught it himself.

In Omaha we stopped in front of a large hotel. "Ten minutes break", said the driver. I went into the Ladies' Room of the hotel, which also had a nice well-furnished lounge. I sat down to start writing a letter, and quite forgot the time, and the coach — my mind was far away. A pat on my shoulder; the smiling face of the coach driver. "Are you coming with us, or staying here?" he asked. They had all been looking for me, and the coach should have left 30 minutes ago. Johnny greeted me with the words: "Look at my new toy. I bought it at Woolworths. I had to buy it because I had too much money left. I had 30 cents and there are only two more days to travel. How could I manage with 30 cents for two days? I had to spend 10 cents."

Arriving very tired in Denver after that long but interesting trip, I had some days rest to catch up on my sleep, and then was lucky enough to find employment in the national Jewish Hospital there. I was assigned to a women's ward; but soon transferred to the children's section. And here is where I felt at home and happy. The first morning when I came into the ward at 7.00 am my colleague said: "The first thing we do is give every child a sponge bath. Have you nursed children before?" "Oh yes!" "Then you know what to do." Well, I knew what to do. There was a little handbasin in one corner of that ward. I went to one of the beds. "Billy", I said, "I am going to give you a ride." I wheeled him - that is his whole bed - over to the washbasin. "Now, help yourself, Billy. This is the cold water tap, this one the hot one, here is your flannel, here your towel, now get busy. In five minutes I will call for you. And then somebody else will have his turn." I got permission from the doctor to have them sit on blankets on the floor, so they could play games together.

This was a TB hospital and these children had TB of the bones - and were in plaster casts. Most of the children had casts on their hips and legs, therefore could not stand up or walk, but as soon as they were allowed on the floor - children are inventive - they got on their stomachs and moved like snakes and even had races all through the ward. Once in a while one of the casts suffered a crack, but that was always repaired

55

quickly. I am sure that the physical exercise was beneficial for those children; one could tell by their enthusiasm.

———

In May 1939 my sister and brother arrived in New York. As they stepped off the boat they had two dogs, Happy and Lona, in their arms. My sister put Lona into my arms and said: "A present from father for you." Happy, my father's beloved dog, had his own suitcase with all the things needed for a well-groomed champion, with hand-written instructions from my mother about his nutritional needs. My brother, sister and I moved into two furnished rooms near Central Park, so as to be able to walk the dogs there. The dogs had priority with everything; when I cooked something for dinner, it would be beef for us and chicken liver for them; they wouldn't eat ordinary liver.

On the first day, when I had carefully prepared Happy's dinner, I put it on the floor in the bathroom. Happy went as far as the threshold, and there he stopped, looking first at his dinner, then at me, and finally moved away. My sister said: "He's not used to being served in the bathroom." I took the dish and put it in the sitting room. Happy came, looked at it, and turned away again. "What's wrong now?" I asked. "Take away the newspaper underneath the dish", my sister said, "He's an aristocrat, not a refugee like we are." I took away the newspaper, replaced it with a white towel, and Happy enjoyed his dinner.

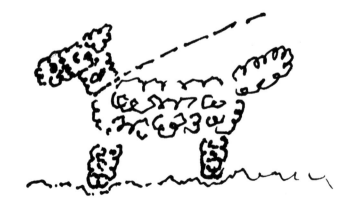

CHAPTER 4

WORLD WAR TWO AND AFTER

War work

SOON AFTER THE WAR STARTED, the government offered short training courses, one for Inspector for Precision-Tools and Instruments. I went for an interview. The conditions to be admitted were: a higher education, four years of university, and at least two years higher mathematics. I told the interviewer: "My years of studies were twenty years ago. I don't remember much of it." She assured me: "It will all come back to you quite easily when you hear it again." I wondered, how could it come back when I had never heard it. 'But I will take the risk', I thought, 'If they cannot use me, they will chuck me out.'

The course lasted thirty days. We learned to draw blueprints, to read blueprints, to work from blueprints. We learned to handle and use all kinds of tools and precision instruments. The first day, as I entered the classroom, there were two black girls sitting in the front row, with some empty chairs between them and the white people, who were mainly middle-aged academics. I sat down next to the black girls to bridge the gap. The next day only one of the black girls was there. When lunchtime came I invited her to have lunch with me. From that time on I was boycotted by everyone. I had joined that course because I wanted to help fight the Hitler regime. Now I was also fighting colour discrimination in this class.

And strange as it was, I also seemed to be in a minority otherwise. The following happened often: the instructor would read a statement and say: "Everybody who thinks that this statement is right put up their arm." All arms went up except mine. I called out: "Wrong", and the instructor said: "Sorry class, Miss Karger is right." Or all the class might say: "Wrong" and I called out: "Right", and the instructor said: "Sorry class, Miss Karger is right."

At the end of each week there was an examination and some students were told (advised) to leave and join the course for working on the assembly line. After four weeks we were only ten students left of the original twenty-five for the final exam. It was a tough exam, including theory and practice, and lasting over several days. I passed, and now I had a qualification in the USA. I was an Inspector for Precision-Tools and Instruments, and could look for a job as such.

My first job was in a large factory. I was hired as 'inspector', but when I arrived was told that everybody had to start as a 'cleaner', drilling holes into metal pieces. We were more than 100 workers in one large room. I was shown to my work bench. There was no chair. I looked around, spotted an empty chair, hurried to get it, but found it chained to a workbench. And then the foreman informed me that I had not earned the right yet to have a chair, not for the first six months. Then I found a wooden crate, but the foreman took it away from me. He explained: "You may have that after two months." I stayed at that job for one month.

My next job was in a very small factory. There was not enough work to be done. We sat idle part of the time, but were told by the foreman to pretend to be busy whenever the manager passed by. I left after one week. My third job as inspector was with the US Navy. My work there was diverse and interesting. I felt very honoured to be put in charge of the tool crib beside my regular work. The conditions under which we had to work were not ideal (stuffy hot rooms, closed windows, no air-conditioners, no ventilators, metal-dust and the noise of the machines). I stayed on this job for over a year until the navy cancelled the orders and the factory closed down.

Once, while working in this factory, I felt weak and faint. The foreman sent me up to the factory nurse. She offered me aspirin. "No", I said, "I need fresh air." "I will give you some tablets, that will help you." "I want to get out into the fresh air. I need some oxygen." Now the nurse wrote a note and handed it to me. "Go out of the building, give this note to the guard at the front door." As I passed the guard I handed him the note. "Wait a minute", he said, "I have to go with you." With the uniformed guard I walked around the block. Then as I wanted to go inside again, he held me back. "We have to walk around the block once more", he said, "The note says 'twice'".

———

It was during this period, in November 1943, that my parents decided to risk the journey across the Atlantic in a convoy. My sister, brother and I knew that our parents had left London, but being in the middle of the war, everything else was kept secret. We didn't know the name of their boat, or when it was due to arrive in New York, but finally the parents did arrive, and the family was joyfully reunited.

———

It was also at about this time that I first came across Mela, the mother of Stefan. He was still an infant when his father died, but she never married again. She really lived for Stefan. She got him through school, through college and through university. Mother and son lived together until Hitler invaded Austria. Then she managed to emigrate to New York, where she had relatives, but Stefan, who by chance was born in Budapest, could not get a visa for the USA and went to Shanghai instead, hoping to join his mother later. In Shanghai the refugees lived under very difficult conditions, mostly in damp and cold rooms. Having been a polio victim some years before, Stefan could only walk with the help of crutches, so he couldn't use public transport. He was unable to find work, but his mother, who supported herself by sewing leather gloves, sent him a cheque every month. The longer she was separated from Stefan, the more she fretted to see him. I visited Mela regularly, felt very sorry for her, and wondered how I could help. It turned out that there would be a way to get Stefan into the USA: a wife in the USA who claimed him, or a fiancée who would marry him as soon as he got off the boat. I wrote to Stefan and offered to marry him, suggesting that we could divorce again after six months. Stefan accepted my offer.

We filled in all necessary forms, and he passed his final health examination. He wrote to say he had got his ticket, and was looking forward to leaving Shanghai in three weeks. Then there was no further mail from him. 'Maybe he is on his way', I thought. His mother was very worried. I tried to reassure her, but no mail came. She waited and waited; three weeks without any news. Finally a letter came, but the address on the envelope was not written in his hand. In anguish his mother sat down, opened the letter, and a printed newspaper clipping fell into her lap. It simply said that Dr Stefan Raditz, her son for whom she had waited all these years since they had been separated, was dead.

———

After my factory work, I took up nursing in private homes again. Among my employers was a young couple who had immigrated from Belgium. Their grandparents were Orthodox Jews, and everything had to be kosher. When I arrived at their house in New York to take care of the 5-day old baby, I found the father sitting on the floor in the living room surrounded by large trays with cookies, candies, cake and so on. In the bathroom the tub was full of wine bottles. I was told that we would have a big celebration on the next day: the *brith* or circumcision, with 40 guests.

The next day was a bit hectic; the mother was sick in bed, but the guests were asked to put their coats on top of the mother's bed. The baby was dressed up like a prima donna, and all the mother's jewellery was put on him: her rings on a golden chain around his neck, her diamond watch around his arm, and so on. 'Why all this?' I wondered, and the mother explained it was 'to make him more valuable, to make him dearer.' After the prayers and ceremonies the Rabbi performed the operation, with the guests looking on, but a little later the baby came down with a bad infection, so I had to stay on that job for several weeks.

One day, when busy in the kitchen, I noticed an old metal box, the size of a cigarette case, standing on the cooker. I moved it out of my way. The next day it was there again, so I looked inside and then threw into the incinerator what I took to be the old screws that were in it. Later, the baby's father asked me if, by any chance, I had seen his metal box, and then I learnt that what I had thrown out was actually his diamonds: he was a diamond cutter! Luckily he found them again in the ashes. Diamonds, I discovered, do not burn.

———

Another of my cases was a young woman with a new-born baby and a two-year-old child. The family was due to move from New York to Seattle, Washington State. As I had been the maternity nurse for the baby, the young father asked me if I could take on the job of bringing his wife and the two children to Seattle. He would go on ahead to find a house, and wouldn't then need to come back to fetch them. I agreed to help, but since the war was still on, it meant travelling by train for three days and four nights.

A week before we were due to leave, I went to Grand Central Station, from which we would get a direct train to Seattle, to ask if our compartment would have an electric socket I could use for the steriliser for the baby's bottles, and to heat the food for the 2-year-old. We were due to have the whole compartment to ourselves; it had an upper and a lower berth, and a settee on which one could sleep. There was also a tiny private bathroom with a toilet and a washbasin.

I knew we would be on the train for a long time, and suggested to the young mother that we should take sterilised bottles, a supply of powdered milk, and some baby food for the boy which would only need heating up. "No", she said, "I am going to breast-feed the baby, and we'll go to the restaurant car for all our meals. We're not doing any food preparation in our compartment." Nonetheless, I filled a suitcase of my own with sterilised bottles, a steriliser, powdered milk, junior baby food etc. and also tea and instant coffee for both of us.

When we boarded the train I told the porter that we had two small infants and would need a lot of hand towels each day. The good man supplied me with 1½ dozen cotton towels every morning, which I used as nappies for the children. We set off, and after some hours, the young mother found she was unable to nurse the baby, so I was glad I'd taken all the equipment. I fixed up the compartment as a nursery, the baby basket on the upper berth during the day, out of reach of the active little boy. On the wall I fixed a plastic shoe bag with several compartments in which I kept the toiletries and utensils for the care of the baby. I had also got a rubber sheet and basin, so each night both infants got a regular sponge bath. Soon everyone on the train was aware of our mini-nursery, and it became the talk of the train. On the first day, we found that there was a 1½ hour queue for lunch, so I was very glad of the meals for the little boy, which only needed warming up. We managed well, though it was a long ride, very tiring, and trying at times.

At 8.00 o'clock on the fourth morning we finally pulled into Seattle. I expected the father to be on the platform to meet us, but I couldn't see him, so I called a porter. All the luggage was put on his trolley, with the baby in her basket on top, and so we walked along, I trying to keep up with the porter, the mother who was feeling rather ill on my left, and the reins of the lively 2-year-old in my right hand. After four days, he was anxious to work off some of the energy he had been saving up on the train. There was no sign of the father, so I asked the porter to take us to the waiting room. I didn't have the address or telephone number of the new house, so we just had to sit there. After an hour the father arrived, smiling cheerfully when he saw us. "What happened?" I asked. "Nothing", he said, "I overslept." We packed into a car and drove to the new house.

It was in fact a very big old house. The father explained that the furniture hadn't yet arrived from New York, but that would not be a problem. "I was able to borrow the essentials from friends."

We went upstairs to see the bedrooms. The first one, he said, would be his and his wife's. The second would be Johnny's nursery, and the third one would be for the baby, and for me as long as I was with them - I had promised to stay for two weeks to help them get settled. There was an iron bedstead in the otherwise empty room, and I was really touched. 'How nice of him', I thought, 'He's even made up the bed for me.' It looked so lovely and inviting, with a purple silky eiderdown on the bed like a comforter, and nice, clean, starched sheets. The house seemed pretty cold, though, and the father said: "All we have to do is go down to the cellar and shovel coal into the boiler, which will make it nice and cosy, you'll see." There was no food in the house, but again he said: "That's no problem. I'll go out right away and buy some. Just give me a list of what you want."

That first evening, when I went to bed, I jumped up again the minute I lay down. There was no mattress on the bed. The sheet was lying on top of the metal springs. I put the sheets on the floor, and slept there. Next morning, when the father saw me, he greeted me with a friendly but sheepish smile and said: "How did you sleep, Miss Karger?" I just looked at him. "If it's any consolation to you", he said, "I didn't have a mattress either. My friends didn't have any to give us." I stayed two weeks as I had promised; they were nice friendly people but it was really not an easy job.

———

A cousin of mine and his wife also lived in Seattle, and they had invited me to spend the week-end in their house when my time with that family was up. On that Friday, 21st December 1945, my cousin came to call for me, but he brought bad news. There had been a call from New York that my father was seriously ill, and I should come home as fast as possible. As it was still war-time there were no flights for civilians. You had to travel by train, and the travel agent told me that it would take several months before I could get a booking, unless it was an emergency.

I called my brother in New York and asked him to send me an urgent telegram to help me get a ticket. It arrived in the night, and in the morning I went back to the agency. "In a case of emergency I could give you a booking in four weeks," he said "but it is not an emergency as your father has not died yet." I was determined to leave that same day, and if I could not get a ticket, I would leave without a ticket. In the evening I went to the station. I walked right through the gate and on to the train. It was a military train, soldiers who were going home on leave. They were in high spirits. I was the only woman on that train. The guard gave me a berth; it was an upper berth.

When I wanted to get down in the night I found the ladder had been taken away. I tried to ring the bell, but the bell didn't seem to be working. I asked the soldier who was lying under my berth if he could get the porter for me. He said: "The porter isn't here; he is in the next carriage." I said: "Can you get a ladder for me?" He said: "They took the ladder away. This is wartime, Miss." "How about the bell?" "This is war time, Miss. The bell doesn't ring." I asked him: "Would you advise me to try to jump down?" "No", he said, "No, don't try to jump; you'll surely get hurt if you do. We'll help you." And so they did, and afterwards helped me up again.

When we reached Chicago on the Tuesday, we had half an hour before the train left again. I ran to a phone, and told the operator: "This is an emergency. Can you put me through to New York?" She said: "If we are lucky, in three hours." "I said: "That's no good, my train leaves in half an hour." "Wait a minute", she said, "I'll see what I can do." I heard her talk to the New York operator, and half a minute later I heard my mother's voice on the phone. "How is father?" I asked. She said: "I don't know." I said: "Can he still talk?" She said: "You'll be here soon, you can see for yourself." I knew what that meant. Father had died the day before, on Christmas Eve.

———

The next two months I stayed with mother in her little flat. I took on nursing cases where I only had to work in the day time, and could go home to mother in the evening. Through all of 1946 I nursed in private houses, and then, on the 26th December, I received a phone call from Los Angeles. "Lenny here. We had a baby today, six weeks too early. Can you come and take care of her?" I said: "Look, I can't tell you right now. I'm here on a case where I promised to stay three weeks, but maybe I can leave a little before. Call me back tomorrow and I will tell you."

The new baby was the little sister of two boys that I had taken care of in New York some years earlier. On the last day of December I boarded

63

a plane and flew to Los Angeles. At that time there were no jets, and the trip took 12 hours from New York. It was my first flight - I had never been in an aeroplane before, and I wasn't so sure what to expect, so I prepared myself well for the flight. I put on a pair of Oxford shoes going up right over the ankles. I thought if we have an accident and the plane goes down, I don't want to sprain my ankles. But the plane didn't crash. It was a beautiful flight, and I was delighted.

I took with me from New York one of our two-month-old puppies, a long-haired dachshund who was going to make his home in Beverly Hills, where the family I was going to already had one of our dachshunds and had wanted a second one. When I boarded the plane with the dog in his container, I enquired if the room, in which the container would be put with all the baggage, was heated, and as they told me it was cold, I refused to let the dog go in it. I said the dog must travel with me in the plane. It happened that the seat next to me was vacant, so as soon as we were in the air I took Peter, the puppy, out of his container and sat him on the seat next to me. He was very well behaved, and liked by the passengers and stewards. They even gave him a hamburger for his lunch.

We circled over the hills around LA - it was beautiful. Snow covered the hills, and we landed with the New Year bells ringing. There was Lenny, my friend, embracing me with the words: "It's good that you are here." We drove home to his house where Sylvia, the young mother, was. "Where is the baby?" I asked. "In the hospital", she said. "She is underweight, and the hospital rules are that they keep the infants there until they weigh five pounds." I objected, and said: "No, I am trained for dealing with premature babies, and know what to do. I want the baby at home." Sylvia looked at me and smiled. "Here is the number of the paediatrician. You can fight it out with him. He is the doctor and you are the nurse. I am only the mother - I have nothing to say."

The next morning I called up the doctor, had a good talk with him, and the same afternoon Lenny and I went to the hospital and got the baby. I installed a home-made incubator, and I kept the baby in strict isolation. Only in the afternoon at 4.00 pm could the baby be 'seen'. Then her father, her brothers, the dog, friends and neighbours stood in the street in front of the window, where she was held up. Everything went well.

A friend of Sylvia also had a new baby, but in her house things did not go so well. George, her husband, came for advice. He said: "We have had six nurses in six days. Nobody wants to stay. Our new baby is screaming. David (2 years old) is fussing, my wife is crying and Grandma is shouting. The Registry refuses to send us another nurse." Sylvia said: "Ilse, you better go over there to help them. I will try to manage alone." "No", I protested, "I will not leave you. But tell George to bring his baby here. We can take care of her for three weeks, so that his wife can take a vacation."

An hour later our boarder arrived with all her 'entourage'. George handed me a box with phenobarbital pills. "What's that for?" I asked. "She gets it three times a day", he said. "Not in our house; take it home." Then he handed me a syringe. "What for?" I asked. "She gets it after every meal." "Not in our house; take it home." Then he gave me her formula. 'A starvation formula', I thought. As the last thing, George carried in a large, heavy, covered saucepan. He explained: "I brought you a pot with boiled water to make it easier for you." After three weeks we sent her home: a healthy, thriving baby. All she had needed was the right formula and a good atmosphere.

Seven months later I took the three neighbour's children in with our three children and made it a kind of children's camp for two weeks to give Sylvia, Lenny and their neighbours a vacation together without the children. The children, being neighbours, knew each other, and they were about the same age. So for two weeks I took care of two 5-year-old boys, two 4-year-old boys, one infant of 7 months and one infant of 3 months. The conditions I made were: no cleaning woman during that time, as I wanted the children to have access to every room in the house, and no visitors — no grandmothers either.

When I offered to take care of these six children, Sylvia said: "Do you know what you are in for? Michael never stays in his bed in the evening. He runs all over the house until late at night." And Peggy from next door said: "My boys are very poor eaters. And my four-year-old gets out of bed at 5.00 or 6.00 am, and empties all the drawers in the whole house on to the floor. I advise you to tie a rope around the chest of drawers to prevent that. And my baby has to be rocked to sleep, her crib has to be rocked sideways." "Leave it to me", I said, "I will manage."

That first evening when I had put the children to bed, I told them: "There are some rules in this camp. Listen carefully. It's alright for you to get out of bed but you cannot get back into your bed again for this night. Another rule is: anyone who is noisy after I turn off the light has to leave his bedroom." "Where will I sleep then?" asked Michael. "I don't know, you would have to find yourself a place, maybe on the floor in the dining-room." "But how about the babies, if one of them cries?" said Michael. "It's the same for them", I said.

Helen, the neighbour's 3-month-old, screamed the first evening. After some minutes I took her out of her crib and put her on a blanket on the floor in the sitting-room. There she went right to sleep, and I carried her back to the crib. For two more days it was the same. After that she went to sleep in her crib without demanding to be rocked. Well, the four boys were very nice. They never left their bed, and they were never noisy in the evening. The chest of drawers was not tied up and the drawers were never turned over or emptied. No fuss was made over the meals; everything was eaten that I served. I can really say the whole venture was a success.

The two couples spent a lovely holiday together. Those four little boys had a grand time, the two infants did very well too, and I enjoyed it. When Peggy came back, she looked at her sleeping baby, and then asked: "And where is my baby?" Her baby looked so well that she had not recognised her. "And my boys look so well, what did you do with them?" she asked. At that time, the so-called self-demand method was very much in fashion, ie one didn't feed the infants according to a set schedule every 3 or 4 hours, but whenever the babies themselves wanted it, and I found that most of the time, after the first three days, the new infant had worked out a very good routine, and came regularly for his meal.

———

After that I was very busy; Dr. Krieger, Sylvia's paediatrician, recommended me to many families, and in between cases I lived at Sylvia's house, which became my headquarters. Also during those two years I became very active politically. Lenny and Sylvia were very active, and living in their house, in the midst of their friends and their activities, I also got caught up in it, especially in 1948 before the presidential election. This was a very busy period for us. At that time I was working as a private nurse in a very plushy, elegant, right-wing house as a maternity nurse. In my time off from 2.00 to 5.00 pm, I would take off my white uniform, get into my trousers, and stand at a card table on Sunset Boulevard trying to get a petition signed for Governor Wallace, the Democratic candidate. I also participated in a large civil rights demonstration when eleven movie people were jailed. We picketed the court-house with big placards. One day, as we walked round it with our placards, there were press photographers on the steps, and as we walked by in single file, they photographed everybody. When I got home, I said: "Today our photos were taken for nothing twice over, first because we weren't criminals and second because we didn't have to pay for them."

On Sundays, when I wasn't on duty, I went with a group of colleagues to the district where the black people lived, and there we went from door to door and sold the Daily Worker. At first I found it very difficult to do that. Never in my life had I sold anything, and now I was asked to go from door to door, ringing the doorbells, and trying to sell people a Communist newspaper.

———

In 1947 I was on my way to a new case, as maternity nurse in a private house in Beverly Hills. I arrived in front of the home. What an estate! What a large elegant house! I checked the address in my hand once more. Yes, I thought, that seems to be right. I took a deep breath, and then rang the bell. A butler opened the door. He looked at me questioningly. "I am the maternity nurse", I said. "Not here", he said. I showed him my slip from the agency. "Oh", he said, "You want that little house over there", and he pointed to a small building in the same grounds but further back in the garden. Well, that was where I <u>was</u> expected.

Here I found a young couple with a new-born infant in a converted garage. It had been let to them as a four-room flat. What a flat! The new furniture for the nursery was standing in the garden covered with canvas as there was no space for it inside the garage. There was a bedroom, a very narrow sitting room, a very narrow kitchen, a primitive shower — no bathroom but a toilet the size of a telephone booth. I was confronted with a sick mother, a sick infant, and difficult circumstances. For instance, when I carried a tray with food from the kitchen to the bedroom, I had to ask the husband: "Please step out into the garden so that I can pass through with my tray."

The first morning the young mother called me into the bedroom. "Miss Karger", she said, "Go to the toilet." I looked at her. "Go to the toilet quickly! My husband went out to get a newspaper, and you can only go to the toilet when he is not at home. The toilet is so small a room that one cannot close the door when sitting down." After three days the sick mother had to go back to the hospital. John, her husband, came to me after taking her there. "Miss Karger", he said, "I have to ask you to leave. I had to pay the hospital for two weeks in advance, to get my wife in. I will have no money to pay you at the end of the week." "I am not leaving; you cannot go to work and at the same time take care of the sick baby. Never mind the money." I stayed on. I really admired this young couple, who in spite of all difficulties and tribulation had kept their sense of good humour and seemed so happy. After I left them, John sent me a small cheque every week. He insisted on paying my full salary, though he earned very little and paid a high rent for that 4-room 'flat' on the rich man's estate.

———

Towards the end of my stay in California I really felt very lonely and I thought it would be a good idea for me to get married, so I went to an Agency to get acquainted with a suitable companion. Yes, they gave me an address and here again I had a very bad experience. To cut a long story short I only have to say that he was a swindler. We had been acquainted for several weeks or months. We had already set a wedding date and we had planned a week's holiday after the wedding. Everything was arranged, when, three or four days before the wedding, I found out that he had an involvement with another woman, and so of course I broke it off right away.

I must say that I was really glad that I had found him out before I got married to him, and not some time later. At that time I was staying with a friend. The day after I broke off the engagement, my friend's mother came to visit her and as she entered the house, she said to me: "Ilse, I am so glad to hear the news. I really want to congratulate you". I just looked at her and said: "What do you want to congratulate me for? For my engagement, or for my divorce?" She looked at me. I said: "Yes, you know I am a fast-working person. Other people get divorced long after they get married, but I already got divorced before I got married." And my friend who was standing by said: "Ilse, I really admire your sense of humour, that you can still make jokes about it." And that was my last involvement with men.

J.K.

68

CHAPTER 5

AUSTRALIA

I HAD LIVED AND WORKED in California for the last two years. On my doctor's order I was to give up nursing and working with children, so I decided to visit my brother, whom I had not seen for 12 years. Honolulu was my first and only break on that long flight. I had intended to stay there for one week. When I got there it was pouring with rain, and when I asked the friendly hotel manager what the weather prognosis was, he said with a smile: "Oh, this is just the beginning of the rainy season. It will last for six weeks."

The following morning I went back to the airport and took the next plane to Sydney. On January 4th I arrived in Sydney. It was cold and wet. The airport was flooded. I walked to the railroad station and took a train to Kogarah. There I queued up for a taxi that was to take me to Kogarah Bay, to my brother's cottage. It took the taxi driver a long time to find that little new street; there were no street lamps, no sidewalks, no pavements and only two cottages at the end of that street.

We had finally arrived. The taxi left. Here I stood in the pitch dark. By now it was 10.30 at night. No lights were on in the cottage. I tried to find the bell. There was no bell. I found a knocker on the front door, but they did not hear me. Then I knocked on the windows. Now a light was turned on, and I heard my brother's voice: "Don't open the door", he said, "At this time of the night it can only be thieves." "It's me, it's me, your sister from America." Finally Louise, his wife, opened the door. "You are six days too early. You have some nerve to do that." And then Rudi, my brother, came. "You did not even give her time to make up her face." That was the reception I got.

———

I had been only two or three weeks in my brother's house when I happened to see a little note in a daily newspaper that the Sydney Day Nursery Association had to close one of their branches, one of their big nursery schools for children of working mothers, because they did not have anybody to run it. I felt that was a pity and thought: 'That nursery school, I am sure, is very badly needed.' So I went to the main office and offered my help. The secretary's first question was: "What Church are you affiliated with?" "None", I said, "When there will be one Church for all people then I will belong to it." "What is your religion?" was the next question. "I am agnostic." "Oh no", she said. Her face lost its colour. "Maybe I did not express myself right. You see, I am of Jewish descent. I am Jewish but a free thinker." She recovered. "Then you are Jewish. That is alright, as long as you are something."

Now I was briefed on the nursery school and given a key to look at it, as she doubted that I would want to work in 'that place' as she called it. It was on the outskirts of Sydney, had been erected in wartime by American soldiers as an army camp, and was now used for slum clearing. Several hundred families lived there in wooden barracks with tin roofs. The former mess-hall was now the nursery school. There was no tree, no bush, no grass. It was like a desert, sand and mud, surrounded by a high wire fence with barbed wire on top.

Rudi and Louise had come with me to look at the place. It was a dirty place. "Oh no", said Louise, "You cannot work here! Look at that filth." My answer was: "I will take on the job because this place needs to be cleaned up." I went back to the office in town, got all my orders and instructions and became 'Director of Herne Bay'.

The instructions were: The nursery school can take in only 50 children. Children who have been in before we closed have to have priority. The hours are from 9.00 to 3.30. The children get a Bostonian lunch. They bring their own piece of fresh fruit in a paper bag. Be careful not to get their fruit mixed up, write their names on their bags as soon as they come in.

On the day of admission there was a long queue. The fourth or fifth woman in line held a small, very frail-looking child in her arm. The child's face was buried in the mother's shoulder. The woman's own face was drawn. She looked old and worried. In a low voice she asked, "Do you take children like her?" "What is wrong with her?" "She is blind." And then I heard this woman's very tragic story. This little girl had all of a

70

sudden become blind after she had had the measles. Her little brother died of meningitis, within eight days. The father could not face up to his son's death. He, the poor woman's husband, walked out of the house and was never seen again. The woman was left with the blind little girl. There was no money in the house, no food, and she was pregnant again. Yes, she had tried to bring the child to the nursery school, so that she could look for a job. But the nursery school had refused to admit the child.

I called up my main office and reported this 'needy case'. I was told not to accept the child. I did not have the heart to turn this woman away. I admitted Pat; I did not put her on the books. 'If I have 50 children on the books, I can afford to have one extra child as a private guest', I thought. Some weeks later the supervisor made her inspection visit. She noticed Pat. She got very agitated. She said: "Miss Karger, we told you that our nursery schools are only for normal children." My answer: "Mrs. Morris, this child is normal, she just cannot see." Mrs. Morris then said: "I will bring it up in our Board Meeting next week; you will hear from us." I never heard a word about it again. But those supervisors! At her next inspection visit Mrs. Morris criticised me because I was wearing wool trousers instead of the director's cotton uniform. "It's not befitting for the director", she said. And when I explained that it was very cold and draughty in that room, she suggested that I wear my trousers under the cotton uniform and pin them up with safety pins.

I ran the nursery school according to my own ideas, and it ran very well. From the very first morning there was a big bowl standing near the entrance door and the children were asked to put their fruit into it, but there were also children who could not bring any fruit. In the afternoon, though, every child was served a plate with mixed fruit, to their delight. Lunch: I had found out that Bostonian lunch meant one cracker with cottage cheese and a glass of milk. I thought that the children of working mothers, who came home from work in the evening tired and had a big family and little money, should have a good meal in the nursery school. I gave them meat, potatoes, vegetables and dessert. I would clean the vegetables and potatoes in the afternoon after the children had left. And the cooking did not seem to be any trouble. The children in turns helped to cook the pudding. They were a happy group. After four weeks I called the first 'Mother's Meeting'. About 15 mothers came. We sat in a circle. I gave a little talk. Then I asked for questions, any kind of questions.

Mrs. Smith was the first one to speak. "Miss Karger", she said, "I noticed that you have a much better class of children here now. How is that?" "Yes, I will tell you, Mrs Smith. We scrubbed the place and cleaned up the children and now they are a better class." I built up friendly relations with the grocery store, with the butcher, and with the greengrocery store, all of which were in the camp, and they all served us very well. There was also a Red Cross Station in the camp, and we visited the very nice Sister with all our little aches and pains, which she was always ready to attend to.

Some of the children are still very vivid in my memory. There was Barry. Very sure of himself, very determined, but he was a poor eater. I always had to feed him his dinner. Then one morning, when his mother brought him, she was in tears. And she explained: "For eight days I have been trying get these glasses on his nose, but he will not let me. He throws them right off. They are correction glasses." "Leave them with me", I said, "I will see to it." And at lunchtime, I took the glasses and handed them to Barry. "Here Barry, put your glasses on, then you can eat much better." From that day on Barry was the first to be finished with his lunch.

Then there was Sherryl, a sweet little girl of four. When the mother brought her in the morning, Sherryl was crying. She also cried in the afternoon, when we put her down for the 'rest hour'. After two days I questioned her mother about it. The mother's response: "Just ignore it, Miss Karger. She has been coming to this nursery school for two years. She is always crying the whole way." That same afternoon, when she was put down to rest and started to cry, I talked to her. "Sherryl, you have to stop. You have no reason to cry. There is no crying without a reason." And Sherryl did stop. The next morning the mother reported that Sherryl had told her that she had not cried in the nursery, and when the mother asked her why not, she had said: "Miss Karger said 'no crying without a reason.'"

Another was Ian. His mother approached me for advice. She could not make him drink orange juice. By doctor's orders he was to have the juice of two oranges every morning. I told the mother to bring the orange juice with her each morning and just put it on my desk quietly. And then, every morning as soon as everybody had settled down, I took care of it. "Come here, Ian." I handed him the glass. "Drink your medicine." Two minutes later he handed me the empty glass.

Another problem was George. His mother told me at the first interview: "George is 4 years old. He does not speak yet, not at all. We thought that he was deaf. He was in the hospital for several weeks but they couldn't find anything wrong with his ears. They do not understand why he cannot talk. I have been trying hard every day for two years to make him talk." When I asked her in which way, she explained that every day in the evening, when George was ready for bed, they looked together at his big picture book, that beautiful book with all the animals. On the first page there is a horse, and she says to George: "Say horse." But he does not say anything. She says it again, but he does not say it. And after she says it for the third time and does not get an answer, she hits him on his fingers with a ruler. And this was the way they had been going through the whole book every day for the last two years.

The next morning George was brought to the nursery school. As soon as his mother had left, I took him and Freddy, a very friendly boy, to a small room to look at all the toys in there together. No sooner had I closed the door behind me when I heard George say: "Freddy, build me something." He said it with a clear and healthy voice. For about four weeks George only spoke when there was no adult in the room. Later I found out that he was a very lively child and quite mischievous at times.

The first thing that I did for Pat, the little blind girl that I had admitted against the orders of my superiors, was to buy her a pair of black glasses. "Look Pat", I said, "here is a nice present for you: sun-glasses just like mine." I let her handle mine and then hers. "Now we will both have sun-glasses." She was so proud of her 'sun-glasses'; it seemed to make a bond between her and me right away.

Very soon Pat adjusted to the life in the nursery. Then one day at the dinner table as she banged with her spoon on the table, I asked her "Stop that", but she kept it up. "Pat, you have to stop that; you cannot do that, eat your dinner." But Pat did not stop, and I asked her to leave the room, showing her the way out. Two minutes later she came back in. "I will not do it anymore." "Then sit down and eat." My helper reproached me: "How could you be so cruel to send a blind child out of the room?" The next morning when the mother brought Pat, she asked to see me. I took her into my office, prepared to receive a complaint. And Mrs. Thomas, Pat's mother, said: "Miss Karger, yesterday was the happiest day of my life. It was the first time that Pat was treated as a normal child, that no allowance was made for her being blind." Pat had told her mother exactly what had happened.

Pat fitted in very well to the daily routine of the Nursery School. She participated in all the activities, she was a happy lass. As she had adjusted so well, we, my helper and I, sometimes forgot that Pat could not see. Once, after some days of heavy rain, the sun was shining and I said to the children: "Everybody take a chair and carry it outside. We can sit outside. I will tell you a story." Two or three minutes later I heard a splash. I turned around. There was Pat floating in the sandbox, which was filled with rain water. While I changed her into dry clothes I asked her: "Pat, how did that happen?" And her answer was: "Honestly and truly I just didn't see it."

How vividly I remember Pat, even now after all these years. Once, just before dinner she asked me, "Is today tomorrow?" "What do you mean Pat?" "Is today tomorrow?" "What do you mean?" "Is today tomorrow?" "Pat, why do you ask me?" "Because yesterday you said, 'Tomorrow it would be my turn to serve the dinners'. Is that today?" Yes, it was Pat's turn. But how could a totally blind child do it? It was a large room, where the children were all seated at small tables, four to each table, and I dished out their dinner at one corner of the room onto each plate, and put it down on a table next to me, from where the appointed servers picked it up to carry it to the children. I wondered how Pat would manage. Pat picked up the first plate and called out: "Who wants some dinner?" And then she walked straight to where that voice came from. "Freddy, here is your dinner." Then she came back for the next dinner. "Who else wants some dinner?" and so she went on.

Once I had invited Pat and her mother to visit me over the weekend in my brother's cottage. That Saturday, early in the morning, Pat asked her mother: "Are we going now?" "No Pat, I have to do the laundry first", said her mother. And Pat exclaimed: "Oh, Mummy, I wish I was a bird!" "What would you do if you were a bird?" "I would fly to Miss Karger's house, and I would not have to wait for you to take me there on a bus."

When Pat was four I took her to the beach, for the first time in her life. She loved it. She would walk into the water, stand there facing the sea, and every time when a big wave had wet her up to her shoulders she would say: "Do it again, do it again, Miss Karger, turn the water on." Pat believed that I was in control of the ocean.

At the age of six Pat entered a boarding school, run by the Catholic Church. She liked the school. Weekends she spent at home, where I sometimes visited her. On such an occasion she suggested that we play school. Her mother and I were to be two of the children, Pat was Miss Green, the person in charge. It was evening, and we, the children, were put to bed. Miss Green said, "Good night, and no more talking after I turn off the light." Out went the light, out went Miss Green. And I started to sing and carry on. In came Miss Green straight up to my bed. "Here is a sweet - and now be good and behave." Miss Green left the room again. And now the other child called her: "Miss Green, Miss Green." Miss Green came dashing in again. "And what is it now?" she asked. "Miss Green, I want a candy also, you did not give me a candy", said her mother. "You don't need a candy, you are good anyhow", said Miss Green, and out she went!

As Pat developed so well, she became the talk of the town; everybody heard of her. Newspaper reporters came to interview me and see what she was doing. So the Blind Institute became aware of it. They approached me one day and asked me if I would consider opening up a nursery school for totally blind pre-school children for them. I told them that I wouldn't do it as a Day Nursery School, that it would only be successful if we could do it as a Boarding Home. I also suggested that we would take in some sighted children, not only totally blind children, because the blind children would later have to be living in a sighted world, and if we took sighted children into the Home those sighted children would set a normal pace and it would be beneficial to the children to get used to living in a sighted world. But the Blind Institute said: "No. We are sorry, but we are the Blind Institute. We can only care for the blind." But still in February 1951 we opened the Victor Maxwell House, a Boarding Home for pre-school blind children.

The house in which we started was a very old, large Victorian house in a big garden. Fifteen high stone steps, without a railing, led up to the front door. The house had once been a hostel for elderly men; it was not really suitable for a children's home, but we started anyhow. We planned to take 12 children altogether, aged from 2 to 5 years, but to allow the children to settle in, and us to get acquainted with them, we took two to begin with, with a further two each week for the next five weeks.

When a new child was brought to us at the nursery, the first thing that always struck us was the child's physical appearance. We were often shocked by it. A lack of fresh air, sunshine and normal activities gave these children a pale, toneless look. The physical state of the children was pitiful. None of them was used to walking without holding the hand of an adult. Their eating habits would remind you of a poorly trained infant. Most children were fed, even at the age of four, from a bottle.

Ilse Karger with Warren at Victor Maxwell House (Sydney, Australia, 1951)

None of them had ever been encouraged to feed themselves. Often they were still on strained baby food, refusing to eat anything solid and spitting out unwanted food. Toilet training was sometimes non-existent; some children of 4 years old were brought to us in nappies. The children were not used to handling or playing with toys — in most cases they had never been offered a toy. They were not used to being with other children either, and so they had poor social skills.

At that time blind children were regarded, by their own families and by the community in general, as sick infants, deserving only of pity, pampering and sham charity. Unfortunately we found that many mothers had a sense of shame about their blind child, and tried to hide it as long as possible from public view. They kept the child indoors and treated it as an infant. We actually had a 5½ year-old who wore a baby coat and was always referred to by her mother as 'Little Julie'.

Initially, Victor Maxwell House had to become a sanatorium as well as a nursery school: before any nursery work could be done we had to build these children up to a normal state of health with massage, oil rubs, a balanced diet, adequate exercise and rest, fresh air and sunshine. Happily we found that the children responded quickly to this treatment, although it took a full year for them to learn the basic movements well enough to be ready for outdoor equipment. We also built up the children's confidence, and their independence. The children learnt to be guided by the voice of an adult; we had no guide rails and we never led children by the hand. No part of the grounds was partitioned off, and they were allowed to roam freely inside the house. They learnt to help us in the kitchen — we treated the children as normal apart from the handicap of not seeing. They learnt to take casual bumps and and falls in their stride without any fuss, and to say with a bright smile: "I'll watch out better next time."

We found that the children were good judges of their own ability, and we never had an accident because a child attempted too much, even though we had swings and climbing bars in the grounds. We never used the words 'Be careful' and we never said 'That's too dangerous.' Self-help was always our aim; for instance, we never carried children up or down the stairs. Those who could not manage to walk by themselves crawled up on hands and knees, or sat and slid down from one step to the next. They became very proud of their achievements; we often heard one child say to another: "I'll tell my Mummy that on Friday."

After we had built the blind children up physically, we took them by tram to the beach once a week, teaching them to get on and off the tram by themselves, having practised this at the terminus. Twice we gave concerts in the auditorium of a large public school. We even entered our children in the annual Eisteddfod competition; it was the first time that pre-school blind children had participated, and our children did very well. This was a big surprise to their parents, and a source of joy and pride to us too.

On Sunday afternnons we had all the children brought back from their weekend at home between 3.30 and 4.00 pm in order to have the parents with us in Victor Maxwell House for two hours. We had an hour of music together, the children playing their rhythm band and singing. We taught the parents a new song each time, and then we served afternoon tea, with the children serving the biscuits. Then the children got ready for their evening meal while I had an informal chat or meeting with the parents, which usually meant talking about their problems of the weekend spent at home. These free talks with the parents as a group seemed quite fruitful, and out of this experience grew my idea of a long weekend, at which the mothers would be our guests at Victor Maxwell House, living in with us and getting 'inside training', so to speak. We went ahead, and it was an eye-opener for the mothers, interesting for us, and the children profited from it too.

As the children became less dependent on adults, we found that their mental attitudes changed completely. The mask-like expression which so many of them wore when we first met them disappeared, and we found that blind children had more courage and confidence in themselves, and the adults around them, than sighted children.

It wasn't easy for me to find the right staff. We started out with a housekeeper to do the cooking, but I found that the food was not suitable for the children, and after I had tried out two or three different housekeepers, I decided that we would be better off doing the cooking ourselves. It was also difficult for me to find the right helper, or carer. Nursery School teachers were not used to dealing with handicapped children, and nurses who are trained to take care of sick infants and sick children again are not used to healthy children. I had employed a young woman who was a trained nurse, trained for sick infants and sick children. I sent her out in the garden with six children and after five minutes she came in crying. I said: "What happened?" She said: "It's impossible for me to watch six children when they are running around in the garden and sitting

on a swing or see-saw." I said to her: "But you are trained for children."
She said: "Yes, I can take care of children when they are sitting in bed,
sick, but not when they are running around in the garden and even sitting on a swing." I said: "I am sorry, but I cannot make a hospital out of
Victor Maxwell House and put the children in their beds so that you can
take care of them." I had to let her go. Then I was lucky to find a very
good assistant in Mrs Harper, a trained children's and infants' nurse and
also a musician. She played very well, and soon after she took over we
had a really good rhythm band, the children playing different instruments,
and she accompanying them on the piano. Of course music plays a big
part in the life of blind children. It really should play a big part in all children's lives, also in the sighted ones.

As I wanted the children to also have contact with sighted children
I formed a relationship with a nearby private nursery school. We invited
a group of children once a week to come over to us for the morning, and
once a week we went over to their place for some hours. But it didn't
really work out. The children from that private nursery school liked our
educational toys in the garden very much. They just played by themselves
and used all our equipment, but they were not willing to play with our
children, so after a while we gave that up. But otherwise Victor Maxwwell
House, was, I think, very successful.

———

In 1951 I received a written invitation to a farewell party, given in
church in honour of the minister, who was leaving after many years of service. I asked my assistant if she would like to go, as one of us had to stay
with the children. "Jean", I said, "You go. It's your church, not mine."
"No", said Jean, "You must go yourself; you got the invitation, you are
the director. They could feel offended." I replied: "I never went to a
church. I don't even know how to behave in a church." "You don't have
to behave at all", said Jean, "You just do what everybody else does."

So I went. I sat down in the very back on the last bench. The church
was crowded. The celebration started. Twelve ministers were sitting in a
row in front, facing the congregation, the one in the middle acting as chairman. He gave a talk, then gave the floor to the minister next to him, and
then to the next again, and so on. They were the ministers of the surrounding districts. After six ministers had had their say, the chairing minister said: "The next speaker on my list is Miss Karger, whom you all
know, if not in person, then by name as the director of Victor Maxwell
House, the new Home for Blind Children."

I felt as if I had been struck by lightning. "Oh no!" I said. But I got up, and very slowly walked up the side aisle, trying to find my bearings. I walked up the steps to the pulpit. There I stood. I surveyed the congregation. I thought: 'They are all very nice proper people. What must I not say here.' And then I started. I did not talk about the departing minister, as that had been done already by those six ministers. But nobody had mentioned the minister's wife. She had been a big support and help to Victor Maxwell House. I said: "When one sees Mrs. Finmont's friendly face, when one sees her blonde hair, and her sparkling blue eyes, it's not hard to like her. But when blind children, who do not see her smiling face and her sparkling eyes love her, then that really means a lot." And I kept on telling the congregation about the close relationship between Mrs. Finmont and the blind children. At the end of that celebration the chairing minister came up to me. "I want to thank you", he said, "I could see that you were well prepared!"

Only eight days after I had been talking to the congregation of the Methodist Church I received a written invitation to be the Guest Speaker at the monthly meeting of the Trained Nurses Association. I went to see the matron of that Association. I asked her about the details. I asked her how long I was supposed to talk, what the title of my talk should be, and I also asked her if I could see the room in which I was going to talk. She showed me the room, and I noticed that there was no table and no chair for the speaker. Knowing that I had a weak back and would find it very difficult to stand up on my feet for a whole hour, I went to a corset shop and got myself a good, strong corset fitted. It was the first time in my life that I was going to be the Guest Speaker. Full of confidence, and with good support, I went there to speak. Great was my surprise when I entered the room and found that there was a table with a vase of flowers, and a nice easy chair for the speaker to sit down. But I found it impossible, with my new, good support, to sit down in that easy chair. So, there was the empty chair standing right next to me all evening. What a pity!

———

After I had been in Sydney for almost a year I remembered that I must have my visa extended. I went to the Immigration Department, put my passport on the counter and when the attending gentleman asked me: "Can I help you?" I said: "I have a tourist visit here for one year. I would like to have it extended." He looked at the passport, looked at me, and said: "You should have left six months ago. What are you still doing here?" I said: "I am sorry, I didn't realise that. I thought it was for a year. "Oh", he said, "And what do you want now?" "I would like to have it extended for another year, because I am working here at a day nursery for working mothers, and I am helping them out. If I didn't, it would have to close, as there is no one else to run it." "Alright", he said, and put a stamp into my passport.

When this next year was up, or almost up, I went to the Immigration Department again. "I am still working as director of that day nursery school in the slums. Could I have another extension?" And without any further argument the stamp was put in. When the third year of my being in Sydney was almost finished I called them up on the phone. "You were kind enough to give me an extension last year. Do I have to come into the office, or could I just send you my passport?" "Oh, we will look it up on the file. Just a minute." After five minutes he came back to the phone. "Oh, yes, Miss Karger, it's alright. Just send me your passport, and we'll send it back."

Then another year was finished. I had now been in Sydney for almost four years, and before I even called up the Immigration Office, they called me up and they offered me British Citizenship. I was stupid enough not to accept. That was one of the big mistakes in my life, which I later regretted very much — as a naturalized American citizen, I couldn't stay away from America longer than five years without losing my citizenship.

———

During one of my vacations, I joined a discussion camp run by Adult Education. We were about fifty people from different walks of life, young and middle-aged, male and female. On the first day we were asked to just line up in a row, then split up into four groups; every group was given a leader and then the assignment was explained. Each group was to put on a show - any kind of show. The show was to last 30 minutes. Every member of the group had to be an active participant in her group's performance. The performance was to be held in three days. A jury would be there as it was to be a competition between the four groups. We were allotted two hours for a discussion within our group to decide and plan, and two hours for rehearsals on each of the following two days.

On that first day each group went off in a different direction, maybe bewildered, maybe anxious. The group to which I belonged, twelve people, were complete strangers to each other and of four or five different nationalities. There we were, thrown together in a somewhat crowded

81

room that served as a bedroom and at the same time as a cloak-room to others. What shall it be? There were many different ideas. Everybody wanted something else. No one seemed willing to listen to anyone else. It was noisy, got noisier as the time went on. There was a lot of talking and debating. Everybody defended his or her own ideas. Our time ran out. We had come to no decision. The same afternoon we heard members of other groups whisper about their projects. We saw people dashing out of camp to get something. Everybody seemed very busy. It did not give us a good feeling.

It happened that I shared a bedroom with our leader. She seemed worried, also angry, and at the same time disappointed. "Wait a minute", I interrupted her, "I have an idea. Let's act what it looks like when twelve strangers are thrown together to put on a show. We will have it easy. We do not need any costumes. We do not need to study or memorise anything. We do not need any rehearsals. We just go on the stage and repeat what we did today. We just act naturally." "OK", she said.

On the day of the competition we were the last group to perform. The first group's performance was a beautiful stage show. We, being part of the audience, admired it - with sinking hearts. The second group did some kind of dance in lovely pastel-coloured paper dresses. I heard voices around me coming from people of my group: "I am not going on the stage; we would be the laughing stock of the evening. Just let us say we did not have anything." The third group was also a good show, and then our turn came. "Come on now everybody", I said, "We have nothing to lose." Someone added: "Because we have lost already."

We went on stage. In the five minutes which were allotted for scene changing I put some nails up, hung up some of the dresses from our bedroom, put my easel and paintbox up. There was also a television and a radio. Then the curtain opened and the play began. One person was reciting a poem while another one was telling him to stop because he wanted us to hear his record. All of a sudden a woman in the audience must have discovered her 'Sunday Best' hanging on a nail on the stage. She came up on to the stage, furious: "I want my dress, I want my dress." I would not let her have it. "You cannot come in here - this is a secret meeting!" After thirty minutes, in the middle of all the noise and confusion, the curtain dropped. We were awarded the first prize because 'it seemed so natural'.

———

Before leaving Australia, in 1953, Margaret, a neighbour had invited us for a day in the country. It was a nice autumn day. She had an old Ford. We were five in the car. She and her sister in the front, two teenagers and I in the back. The car was really not big enough for five, but we were all in good spirits. After two hours of driving we stopped at the roadside for a short break. Margaret suggested that we change seats. She wanted me to sit in the front now, to see more, she said. And as she started the car again, she explained that now I would have to take on a little job. I had to hold on to the gear lever, which otherwise would not stay in place. Every time Margaret wanted to change gear, she just snatched it out of my hand. I was flabbergasted, but managed to keep quiet about it, as I was her guest for that ride.

After 10 minutes it started to rain. As the windscreen wiper did not seem to function, Margaret took one hand off the steering wheel. She tried to fix the wiper. She could not get it going, so she took the other hand off the steering wheel also, and lost control over her car. The car went across the road, hit a telegraph pole, then made a double somersault. It seemed like slow motion on TV. I knew exactly: now the wheels are on top, now on the side and so on. Then down a deep embankment the car went and landed finally on its side. The only noise now to be heard was the car's motor. "Will somebody please turn the motor off", I said. Then they managed to push the door open and they climbed out. I was the last one. I marvelled at that discipline! Nobody talked about her or his own aches and pains. Nobody reproached our driver. Everybody shook hands with everybody. We asked each other: "Did you get hurt?" As we were cold and hungry we decided to have our picnic. Our thermos bottles were unharmed. But the boxes with the cake had been whirled around. We all had chocolate cake and whipped cream in our hair. It looked funny.

While we were standing there, eating and drinking, two men came down the embankment. They had driven a truck and had seen our smashed car. They asked us: "Where are the dead people?" "What dead people?" "The dead people who were in that car?" "We are the dead people", we said. "Stop joking", they said, "This is not a matter for jokes." They found it hard to believe that we had been in that car. From the next village, 25 miles away, they sent us help. The car was beyond repair, but we were not too badly injured. Margaret had a fractured chestbone, her sister a black eye, the 14-year old boy a sprained wrist, his sister a damaged nose, and I had concussion, which led to me spending ten days flat on my back in Margaret's house.

83

After recovering from that, I returned to America. I had to return after having been in Australia for five years in order not to lose my American citizenship, but strangely enough I didn't feel homesick for America. I didn't feel homesick for Germany either. I felt homesick for Italy, where I had lived for two years 25 years earlier, so I took an Italian steamer in order to brush up my Italian before getting there. The boat would take me to Naples.

I knew that I was going to be on the water for 35 days and of course I wanted something to occupy me on the trip. I had seen in one of the big department stores in Sydney that they sold looms; nice looms, all sizes from very big floor looms to little hand looms not larger than a typewriter. They advertised that anybody who bought a loom could learn to weave right there in the department store from a trained weaver, and I enquired how many lessons one could have. "As many as you want", the sales lady said, "As many as you need to feel happy about the weaving." So two weeks before I left Sydney I went to the department store, had my instruction on weaving for one week, and then off I went with my loom.

I got on the steamer in Melbourne. The steamer was very crowded, and I had a berth in the 3rd Class, which meant I had to share it with three other people. I carried the loom in a big cotton bag, with all the material I needed for weaving in a straw waste paper basket, for which I had made a cotton top with a string. When I boarded the ship, I was carrying the loom in front of me, and on my back the waste paper basket with all the coloured cottons. Very soon I was known by everyone on board as 'the lady with the loom'.

In the morning, while the other three passengers in my cabin still slept, I was sitting in my top berth, with the loom on my lap, weaving along happily. Soon I found out that the 1st Class passengers deserted their 1st Class deck in the evening at 10.30 or 11.00. They went in to their salon for dancing, and so I went every evening at 11.00 up on the 1st Class deck. There they had comfortable deck chairs with very good mattresses, and so I made this my headquarters for the night. Every evening I spent the time from 11.00 till 5.00 or 6.00 in the morning on the 1st Class deck, enjoying the beautiful view and having a nice chat with the Deck Steward.

When we came to the South Sea Islands, I got a view which I thought was unique. I had never in my life seen anything like it. On one side of the ocean the sun rose like a big red ball, and just opposite was the full moon, going down. The moon and the sun had almost the same colour: a beautiful orange-red, and for the first minute it was hard to tell which was which. This spectacle I watched for three nights in succession. The first night, in my enthusiasm, I went down to my cabin, woke up the other three passengers, and asked them to come up to the deck and see this spectacle. But they were not interested in the spectacle; they were actually angry, and said: "You have a nerve to wake us up in the middle of the night! Never mind the moon and the sun. We want to sleep!" And back they went to sleep.

When we came to Djakarta, we went ashore. The boat docked there for three hours. We were allowed to go ashore, but we were warned to leave our money and everything in the cabin. I had attached myself to a group of about 20 Boy Scouts and went with them to town where we visited the market. The market was very crowded and we spent some considerable time there. After a while I suggested that I should start on my way back to the boat. I said: "I will go ahead on the main road, and I'm sure in time you'll catch up with me." So off I went.

I walked, and I walked, and I walked, and wondered why the Boy Scouts hadn't come yet. I had the feeling that they should have already caught up with me. Finally, after a long walk, I arrived at the quay, but it wasn't the right one. I had left the main road by mistake and had arrived at the wrong wharf. What now? I had asked people on the way if this was the way to Australia; I meant the boat 'Australia', but the people whom I had asked apparently thought I wanted to go to Australia, and so they directed me to the quay for Australia. I could see my boat far away, but there was water between the boat and the quay where I was, and I couldn't cross the water.

I asked two different cars if they would take me to my boat, but they refused. I asked: "How long will it take me to get there?" and the answer was: "Half an hour." Now I already heard the first whistle of my boat. Off I went. I ran as fast as my legs would carry me. I ran and ran and ran, and finally I arrived at the right dock. At the pass control I wanted to show my passport, but the man said: "No. Run, or you won't catch the boat. Run!" and as I arrived near the boat, the gangway had already been pulled up. The third whistle, the whistle of leaving, had already sounded. What should I do now?

Up on the deck, my deck, I saw my Boy Scouts all lined up in a row, and they were calling down to me: "Hurry, hurry, hurry!" and they were clapping their hands. Now a narrow wooden board was put out of one of the portholes to help me to get on, and I had to crawl on hands and knees on this narrow plank into the boat. It had been my good luck that the Boy Scouts, getting to the boat, hadn't found me. They thought I should have arrived, and when they found I was missing they had gone to the Captain and told him that I was just coming. So they had put out the wooden plank for me. Otherwise I don't know what I would have done, because this was Sunday, when everything was closed, and there I was, in a strange country, not knowing the language and without money. Believe me, I was glad to be on the boat again. Then off we went.

———

Two days before we arrived in Naples, the Steward came to me after dinner and said: "We need you." "What for?" I said. Well, they had seen me sit on the Crew Deck with my paint box painting landscapes in oil. He said: "We need you to paint a mural for us. We are going to have a big party on the last evening on the boat, before arriving in Naples, we have to decorate the big salon, and we want a large mural on the wall to decorate it." I said: "Why do you ask me? Let one of the men do it. You have some men who also do some painting." "No", he said, "We have already tried two men, and what they did we cannot use. We want you."

I said: "Look, I am 51 years old. I don't want to do it. I can't do it." "Yes", he said, "It's very easy for you. Come with me. I'll show you what we want you to do." He took me into the dining room and there on the floor were laid out two big white bed sheets, unfolded. "We want you to fill these two sheets and make a mural out of them. Maybe you can make a picture of a night in Venice." "I am 51", I said, "I cannot lie here on the floor." "You don't have to lie on the floor", the Steward said, "We can pin it up on the wall for you. You can do it on the wall." "No", I said, "It's too much for me to do that here, that late in the evening." "You don't have to do it now in the evening", said the Steward, "You can do it tomorrow after breakfast." "Anyhow", I said, "I wouldn't do it alone. Get me Neil, one of the Boy Scouts, who does some sculpture. He is an artist. Get him." "Where is he?" "Oh, he is in the large dormitory where all the Boy Scouts sleep."

The Steward went to fetch Neil. "Neil", I said, "Look here. See these two sheets? They want us to make a mural." "I am not a painter", he said, "I cannot paint. I only work with clay. I am a sculptor". "All right, I can do the sketching and you can just fill in the colours. If you

help me, I'll do it. If not I will not." "Yes", said Neil, "It might be fun. Why don't we start right now and get it done with?" I said to the Steward: "Where are the paints? What kind of paints are we going to use?" I wasn't going to use my expensive oil paints. "I'll get you what you need", said the Steward, and came back with two little boxes of Woolworth children's crayons. "OK", said Neil, "Let's start." "Neil", I said, "I'm not going to lie down here on my stomach in my good evening dress. I'm going to my cabin to change."

I went down and changed into my bathing suit, and we two lay on our stomachs all night from 10.00 in the evening until 6.00 in the morning. I sketched the Grand Canal in Venice and a lot of little houses along the side of the Canal. I told Neil: "Now you just colour in the houses in light pastel colours, one house light green, the next one pink, the next purple, the next mauve, all in a very light shade. Then you can colour in the water, blue and wavy, and a little white and grey in between." I also put in a gondola, the characteristic of Venice, with a gondolier, and outside, next to the Canal, I put an old-fashioned gas lantern and a couple of young lovers. The man had a mandolin or guitar with coloured ribbons hanging down, the girl had her arm round his shoulder, the moon was shining down on the couple. As time went on we really enjoyed doing it; it was very kitsch.

The next day it was put on the wall, and the Captain came to me, thanked me very much and said: "Usually we use those murals for just one trip, but this time, with such a specially nice mural, we are not going to launder it. We are going to use it for as many trips as possible."

At Naples I got off, as the boat went on to Genoa. When I went through the passport control and the inspection of the suitcases, I asked the officer which one of the cases he wanted me to open. He said to the other inspector: "OK, OK, let her pass. She's a poor artist." And that was my trip from Melbourne to Naples. Thinking of it, I can still see myself on the boat. It was a really exciting, interesting and memorable trip.

88

CHAPTER 6

BACK TO THE USA

I TRAVELLED IN A LEISURELY WAY from place to place through my beloved Italy, and really felt happy to be there again after more than 25 years. Then in the autumn I was back in New York city after five years' absence. What now? How could I find a job? What could I do? Where could I settle down? All these questions were whirling around in my head.

The Lighthouse for the Blind was looking for an assistant teacher for their nursery school, so I went for an interview. The director looked at my credentials. She seemed quite interested. She said: "You have very good references, you have done some wonderful work. I would love to have you work here. But I cannot employ you." "Why not?" I asked. Her answer was: "You would be the person here who would know most about blind children, much more than your superiors. That would not work. I cannot employ you. You are over-qualified for this job."

Eventually I found jobs maternity nursing in private houses, and amongst my jobs was one in the country, with a weekly day off. On one of these days off I decided to go to town. The weather was terrible; it was raining cats and dogs, so I put on my high rubber boots, an old raincoat, took my umbrella, and off I went to the railroad station to catch a train to New York. After an hour's ride, I arrived at Grand Central Station. As I got off the train, the rain was really awful. 'What shall I do here in New York today in this awful weather? It's impossible to go anywhere', I thought, 'But maybe I could find an art gallery not far away. Ah yes, yes, here is a sign 'Art Gallery', and it looks as if you can get up to it without even going out into the street. I'll find out.'

There was a lift inside the station to take one up to the gallery. I found the lift, went in, pressed the button which said 'Art Gallery' and went up, to find myself right in the middle of the gallery in which the exhibition was shown. The room was filled with elegantly dressed people. Nobody was in their street clothes, and here I stood in my dripping raincoat with my big rubber boots and the dripping umbrella. Apparently this was the opening of a show, to which only invited members and the artists who had produced those paintings came. Before I could walk away, a waitress was standing in front of me and offering me a glass of sherry. I took the glass of sherry, put it on the next window sill, and left. It was very embarrassing.

———

Towards the end of that year I was suspected of having cancer. I went to the hospital for some examinations, and was admitted for an operation. I was there for eight days after the operation, lying in a large ward with about 12 beds. There was a friendly atmosphere among the patients. There was one young black woman from the deep south, the only one who never had a visitor as she had no relatives or friends in New York. This was in the 1950s, when the integration of black people had not yet been accepted. Nobody in the ward talked to this young woman, except me.

On the 23rd December the doctor came in and said: "You can go home. You are all right. The test was negative." Strangely enough, instead of being happy and joyful, I felt guilty, very guilty. I felt like saying: 'It isn't my turn yet to go home. I have been here only ten days, and all the other patients in this ward have been here much longer, some of them three months, some six months or even longer. It really isn't my turn.' As I left the ward, I said to the young black woman: "I will visit you." I left the hospital, and on Christmas Day I came back to visit her. As soon as she saw me come in, the young black woman looked at me with her beautiful black eyes and said: "You said you would come, and you did come." She was very happy about my visit, and I felt that this was really the nicest Christmas present that I could have; the joy and happiness I had given to this young woman by visiting her.

———

In January 1954 I took a job as a governess to the little girl of a millionaire in Princeton. They lived in a beautiful big estate; the house had 26 rooms, a large swimming pool and garden, employing several gardeners. I was with that family for almost a year, and I must say that this year was one of the most unpleasant in my life. For one thing, I wasn't allowed to take the child into the swimming pool because I was not an officially certified life guard, though I was a good swimmer and had taught several children to swim. For another, when I arrived in Princeton, they gave me a very tiny room, not even big enough to put a table in. I was told that I would have the room only temporarily, but I was never given another one. On my day off I had to be on duty from 7.00 until about 9.00 o'clock in the morning, so not even on my day off could I sleep as long as I wanted. At 9.00 o'clock the chauffeur would take me to the railroad station and I would go into New York, about an hour's ride, to spend my day off there. Again, I had to be back in Princeton at 10.00 o'clock in the evening. That meant leaving New York at 9.00 o'clock at the latest, so I couldn't even stay for dinner with friends.

In summer the family went to Switzerland for six weeks. We crossed the Atlantic on the Queen Mary, and these 4½ days were very trying for me. I felt like a prisoner isolated in a cell. The child was put to bed at 7.00 o'clock in the evening, and I had to sit in the cabin and watch over her in case she was kidnapped. I wasn't allowed to have a light on in the cabin, because it might disturb her, so from 7.00 until I finally retired myself, I had to sit in the dark. I was forbidden to talk with any of the stewards, because I was the governess of the rich people. However, the rich people wouldn't talk to me, because I was only a governess.

We spent the vacation in a big hotel in Villars, but I wasn't allowed out of the hotel garden with the child until the parents came down. They never came down before 11.00 o'clock. After that we walked together down to the village souvenir store, where the father bought the newspaper and some picture post cards. That was all we got to see of Villars. After a week I asked when I could have my day off, and was told: "You don't expect to have a day off while we are here, do you? You don't expect me to play with the child while I have a governess to do that?" I finally insisted on having at least one full day off before we left again for New York, and we agreed on a day.

That morning it was foggy and wet, but I made it my business to leave the hotel at 7.00 o'clock in the morning before they could notice that I was gone. I wasn't going to lose the chance of having at least one day alone. I left the hotel and went up to the mountains in a cable car, determined to take a good long hike. The rain didn't stop; it got worse, and turned into a bad storm, with thunder and lightning. I walked for several hours until finally I came to a mountain *Hütte* or hostel, which I entered, soaking wet. The owner made me take off my wet clothes, gave me a woollen blanket to wrap up in, and dried my clothes for me. I had promised the family to be back at 6.00 o'clock in the evening, but the owner of the hostel wouldn't let me leave. "You cannot walk down now in this awful weather", he said, "It is dangerous. You'll have to wait until the storm is over."

I decided to call up the hotel, tell them that I was safe and that I would be late on account of the bad weather. Mr Spanel answered the phone, and when I told him that I had to stay until the bad weather was over, he said: "Call for a taxi to come up to the mountain and get you. I will pay the fare." Of course, there was no possibility of getting a taxi up the mountain to collect me, and he was not pleased. All in all, I was glad to leave that family after a year.

———

Then followed some more private nursing and maternity cases in Westchester and New York, and on the 1st March 1955 I started to work in St. Barnabas House, a temporary children's shelter in Bleaker Street, in the slums of New York. There I was working with a group of 4-year old children. The whole house had space for 85 children, grouped by age from toddlers to 14 years old. Half the children were American negro children, 49% Puerto Rican, and 1% white American children. Though I didn't agree with all the rules and regulations in that home, I still liked to work there; I liked the children and I was on the staff for 2½ years, first as a group worker and later as one of the nurses, taking care of the infirmary and sick children.

On one occasion, a dull winter day, we took a group of twenty 4-year-olds on a walk. We happened to pass a church and one of the children said: "We cannot go into the church, can we?" As a negro she was already used to discrimination. "We can go in", I said, "I will have a look to see if it is not too crowded." Before I took the children in I reminded them: "We do not talk inside the church, we do not touch anything, we walk very quietly, one behind the other. I will be the leader, and you all follow me." I asked my young helper to be the very last to come in. Everything went very smoothly until we came to the front. There stood a coffin. What now? We had to pass it. In my thoughts I saw Ricardo, a very lively youngster, beat with both hands on the coffin and say: 'This is how the big Chief Indian beats upon his drum!' And someone might get scared at the sight of that coffin, I thought. I felt they must not see the coffin — but they had to pass it. We had to go on. I turned my face up towards the ceiling. I stared at the ceiling. That way with raised heads we walked on, looking all the time at the ceiling. Nobody saw the coffin. As we came out of the church one little girl remarked: "Wasn't that a pretty ceiling!"

———

When my first year at St. Barnabas House was almost finished, I was told that I had to take my yearly vacation. Of course I wasn't happy about it, but they insisted. But where would I go in March? I like the mountains! But in March? Well, there must also be some mountains in the southern part of the USA, I thought. I got hold of an atlas. My eyes went for the mountainous regions in the south. 'Now my pencil shall decide for me.' I closed my eyes and let the point of the pencil land on the map. 'Nashville' the pencil said. Nashville, a town in the Black Mountains in North Carolina.

It was a very long trip from New York to Nashville by coach, and I arrived late at night. The next morning, on my way to a travel agency, I happened to see a postman. 'He might know a place', I thought, so I asked him, and he recommended Vainsville. "It's a lovely, small place, up in the mountains, and it's easy to get to", he said. "Only one and a half hours with the local bus." Off I went to Vainsville. It was a beautiful drive through the country, real country, with hills and valleys. We passed many small villages. And then we came to Vainsville. But it was a town, like many others in the USA. There was the main street with Woolworth, a supermarket and a post office. On the horizon were the mountains. I was disgusted. I walked in to the Chamber of Commerce and when the lady asked me what I wanted, I said: "I have come to give you a piece of my mind. Are you ready to take it?" "Yes", she said with a friendly smile. "Look", I continued, "I have travelled all the way from New York to be in the mountains. Nashville disappointed me. That's why I travelled on to Vainsville. And again I am in a town. I want to be in the mountains! Where can I go?" She had a list of resorts, and one place she recommended specially: high up in the mountains, 4500 feet altitude. By car about one and a half hours drive. Self contained cottages. "Mr Price would take you there. He would gladly show you the place, even if you would not want to stay there", she said.

Early next morning Mr Price called for me. The drive up to Rosemount was unbelievably beautiful. It really was breathtaking. In the forest the snowdrops were blooming, and violets and dogwood and many other plants. I returned to Rosemount several years in succession. It really was paradise.

93

In June 1956, after an operation, I went to World Fellowship (WFS) for the first time. It was here that I met with Willard Uphaus, the director of WFS, who upheld and fought for human rights and civil liberties, and was to have a great influence on my life. He was a man with great inner strength, and at the same time always friendly and gentle.

Willard had a special rapport with children. One day, as Lili aged six and I were walking through the forest, Willard passed us with his car. "That was Willard", said Lili. "Did you recognise him by his blue car?" "No", said Lili, "Not by his blue car." "By his white hair?" I asked. "No, not by his white hair." "By his blue eyes?" "No, not by his blue eyes." "Then by what did you recognise him?" "By his friendly face!"

Once, two of the guests, both middle-aged women, had a row. One of them went to see Willard and complained. Then the other one went to explain. "Willard", she said, "She really is impossible! I tried to be nice to her, I really tried." "Don't TRY to be nice - BE nice", said Willard.

I remember two other guests at WFS. They were still strangers to each other, and sat in front of the cottage where they got into conversation. They talked about politics, about the world situation, about different things. And then one of them, Mr Gray, said: "How do you feel about negroes?" And Mr Drake said: "Well, you are asking the right person. I can tell how I feel about negroes. I AM a negro." "No, you are not", said Mr Gray, "You are kidding me!" "Why would I tell you that I am a negro if I were not? I really am a negro." "I still don't believe it." "Why not?" "You don't look like one. What is your profession? What do you do?" "I am a taxi-driver" said Mr Drake. "No, you are not", said Mr Gray, "You are much too nice and intelligent to be a taxi driver." "But I AM a taxi-driver!" "Do you like that kind of work?" "Yes, I do. I meet a lot of different people, I can talk to a lot of people - I like people." And Mr Gray concluded: "I still cannot understand how you can be a negro and so intelligent."

———

One day Willard's mother, aged 91, said to me: "Ilse, I have never yet shown you my box of hankies, you know, my old friends." She went to her room and came back with a box. The box was tied up with a pretty ribbon. She took off the ribbon, and as soon as she had taken it off, the lid of the box seemed to lift up by itself, before she moved her hand to lift it. With a bright smile, old Mother Uphaus said to me: "You see, Ilse, all my old friends want to talk to me at the same time."

94

She opened the box and carefully took out one after the other of all the hankies, which she called her old friends. The hankies were of different material; some were linen, some were cotton, some were white and some were coloured. Some had embroidery in one corner, most of them had a nice crochet lace border. Mother Uphaus, with a loving look, opened each one carefully to show me, and she told me who had sent it to her, and on what occasion it had come.

They were all greetings. They came from different parts of the world, and at different times. Some came for her birthday over the years; some were Christmas greetings, and some for other occasions, but she knew exactly who had sent each, and when. After she had shown me all the hankies, she put them back lovingly and carefully, closed the lid of the box, tied the ribbon round it, and carried it back to her room.

———

It was also at WFS that I first met Sylvia and her husband Robert. Both were totally blind. We became good friends, and soon she told me her story. When she was six years old, and her sister was 11, her parents, who owned a restaurant in New York, left the two little girls alone at home, and went to attend to their business. Before they left, the mother told the older one called Alice that she should watch the little one, and take care of her. After the parents left, the children were quite all right for a while, until the little one got hold of a metal tape measure. She found that it was a lot of fun to press the button in the middle and see the metal tape come out, and then let it go back again into the spool. After she had played with it for a while, the sister, who noticed it in her hand, told her to put it down.

But Syl didn't; she kept on playing with it. Now Alice tried to take it away from her, but Syl wouldn't let go, and so they were both fighting for the metal tape. Suddenly the tape sprang out of Alice's hand and into Sylvia's eyes. In due course she lost the sight of her eyes through a bad infection, and became totally blind. Of course the mother got panicky and very upset. She scolded Alice, reproached her for not having watched her little sister well enough. She punished Alice; she told her that since her sister would be blind for the rest of her life, it would be Alice's job and responsibility always to be her sister's companion, always to take care of her. She, Alice, could never get married; she just had to be her sister's guardian for her whole life.

95

Alice and Syl went back to school; they both had a good education, but Syl suffered from believing that she would be a burden on her sister all her life, and she made up her mind that she wouldn't do that. She didn't want her sister to have her whole life spoiled. When Syl finished her education at 17, she walked out of her parents' house, determined to become independent. She went to the Welfare Office and managed to get a grant to train for a profession and become self-supporting. She was able to move into her own flat, received training, and became a fully qualified social worker. Then she got a job in one of the big hospitals in New York, where she worked for a number of years.

One day, in the Social Club of the Society for the Blind, she met Robert, who was also totally blind, having lost his eyesight in the war. They became friendly, and soon decided to get married. When Syl told her parents that she intended to marry, her mother put up a big fight. She insisted that she wouldn't have Robert as a son-in-law, because, she said, he was not a suitable husband for her daughter, for several reasons. These were, first: "He is not rich. You, as a totally blind woman, need a rich man as a husband, who can provide you with all the comforts you need." The second reason was that she was a Polish Jew while he was a Polish Christian. The third reason was that he himself was totally blind. The mother said to Syl: "You, as a totally blind person, need a husband with good sight, who can really take care of you, and do everything for you." They got married anyway, and were a real model of independence. Soon they had their first baby, Lucy.

When Lucy was born, I visited them every week, and was amazed that they managed so well. Syl was a very good mother, housekeeper and hostess. I imagined that their child would be a little slow in her development, since the parents were a little slow in the pace they set, but I was wrong. Lucy became independent at a very young age. One day, when I came to visit, I found Lucy, at that time three months old, sitting in her high chair at the table and, to my surprise, feeding herself. Sylvia explained how that came about: "You know, Ilse, my daughter didn't like the way I was feeding her when she started to have solid food, because when I fed her, the spoon always landed on her face, but not right in her mouth. It got under her nose, or on the cheek, or on the chin, and the baby started to put her hand on top of my hand, to show me the way into her mouth. Then, one day, she just pulled the spoon out of my hand and fed herself."

The parents had very good ideas about how to bring up children, and they gave Lucy a lot of freedom. When Lucy was one year old, she had a three-wheeler without pedals, which she pushed around with her feet. By that time, Robert had taken a second flat, and knocked down the wall between the two to make one big one, which gave the child plenty of space. When she was two, instead of taking her out in the push chair, Robert took her by the hand, and let her walk with him. She knew he couldn't see, and acted as a 'guide dog'. When they stopped to cross a street, she knew exactly when it was safe to go, and he had full confidence in her. When Syl was 43, their second child was born, a healthy boy, and not long after that they moved to the country.

———

Perhaps John aged 10 should have the last word about WFS and its impact on all who stayed there. On his last day at WFS, he declared that he didn't want to leave. "You will be back again next summer", I consoled him. "Yes, I will be here again next summer. I will always come", said John, "Only the trouble is, when I am grown up, WFS will not be there any more." "Why do you say that?" I asked him, and John said: "It will not be needed any more. Everybody will be nice and friendly to everybody anyhow."

———

Back at St. Barnabas House, I was told that I would be getting a volunteer helper. I looked forward to her arrival with some misgivings. It was Sunday afternoon and I was in charge of twenty small children. 'A volunteer? At six o'clock?' I thought: 'I would rather not put up with her - she will come here as a kind of visitor. She will play with the children. She will get them all excited, when they should really calm down and get ready for bedtime.'

On the dot of 6.00 pm the lift stopped on our floor and out of it stepped Edith, a tall lady, very friendly, in a white doctor's coat, wearing her beautiful braids pinned up around her head like a crown. "Are you Miss Karger?" she asked, and went on: "I came to help you. What can I do?" "Maybe you would like to read a story to the children while I start with the bathing", I said. "No!" she said very firmly, "I did not come here to read stories. I came to work! You can read a story and I will do the bathing." Well, that did it, we worked together. We bathed the children, we put them to bed. Edith came every Sunday from 6.00 to 8.00 pm. On the last Sunday before Christmas I said to her: "Next Sunday you will not be here." "Why not?" asked Edith. "It's Christmas Day", I said. Edith just looked at me and then asked: "Are not the children put to bed on Christmas Day?"

———

Then came Easter. Spring cleaning was done in the whole house; in every department, carers and children were very busy. One of my co-workers, in charge of a group of 20 little girls (10 - 12 years old) said to me: "I am finished with all the cleaning and all the preparations for Easter. All the girls' Sunday dresses are washed and ironed. But some of my children need haircuts badly. I asked the Director for some money, but he said: 'No, we don't have any money for such a luxury.' I don't know what to do! The girls look pretty awful, they do need haircuts!" I gave it a thought. "Wait a minute", I said, "Maybe I could talk to my hairdresser. But his beauty parlour is pretty far away. It's on the West Side in Manhattan, on 72nd Street, near the Hudson River. How would you get there?" "OK", Mrs. Smith said, "We would not mind walking. We could make it a half-day excursion. My girls like to walk." "How many girls need haircuts?" I asked her. "Oh, eight to ten I would say." "Well I will try, but I can't promise anything." I went to the public phone. I called up Eric, my hairdresser (Eric and his wife Betty were refugees from Vienna). "Can you cut the children's hair? And can you do it cheaply?" I asked him. "No", said Eric firmly, "I can't do it cheaply, but I can do it for nothing. Tell your co-worker to bring the children at 9.00 o'clock on Saturday."

That Saturday at 9.00 am my co-worker and eight little girls walked up the stairs to Betty and Eric's beauty parlour They had hung a 'Closed' sign on their door, since they were expecting us. A little timidly Mrs. Smith asked: "Can I leave these girls here and collect them later?" "Why?" asked Eric, and she went on: "I had to take out my whole group; I could not leave them at home. I thought I would take a walk with them and then pick these girls up again." "Where are the others now?" said Eric. "Go and bring them up." Well, twenty girls visited Betty & Eric, and all twenty got haircuts. Everyone was asked how she wanted to wear her hair, and after they had had their haircut, they had a little party. They all received a Coca Cola and a chocolate bar. In the evening they all came to my door: "We like your Betty and Eric", they exclaimed. This was 1956. Integration was still in its infancy.

———

On several occasions I had had arguments with the Director of St. Barnabas House, and we were not on good terms when I left. Two years later I entered the building to visit a former colleague. Against my wishes, the receptionist informed the Director that I was in the building, and he invited me to have lunch with him. I felt I should not turn down his friendly gesture.

98

While we had lunch he said: "We are going to have a staff meeting at 2.00 pm. I would like you to stay on for it." We went down for that staff meeting. The Director introduced me: "Meet Miss Karger; she worked here for over two years. She never followed any of the rules or regulations, she always did what she wanted to do, but she is a damned good nurse. And now I will ask her to tell you something about her work with blind children in Australia. That will be more beneficial for you than a lecture by me." I was given the floor and I had to face it.

———

While working in St. Barnabas House, I used to go on my weekly day off to a State Hospital as a volunteer, and there I set up big looms for the occupational therapist because the patients could learn to weave, but they couldn't thread the big looms. The hospital was very grateful for my coming. They had plenty of volunteers, they told me, but nobody who wants to thread looms because that was very tedious. I did it for several months, and was always received there with joy by some of the Italian patients, who didn't speak English and were happy to have someone to chat with in Italian. Unfortunately I had to give up the work when I was no longer well enough.

After giving up the job in St. Barnabas House, I took myself down to South Carolina to nurse a very sick woman in a private house. Her cousin, a friend of mine, had begged me to take on the job for a little while, thinking that I would be able to lift the patient's spirits. She had been in bed for several years, paralysed from the hips to the toes and bedridden. She was badly depressed, so to do my friend a favour I went down. It was a hard case, heavy physically, but they had a very good cook in the house, who was always willing to give me a hand whenever asked. The town itself wasn't particularly pretty; there was a strong division between the poor blacks and the whites who all owned the stores and lived in good financial conditions. I was the only white person to be seen walking in the streets beside the black people. No white person would walk; they all had their cars.

After that I went back to New York; my cousin Fritz, who was in his late 70s and had Parkinson's disease, was living there and being looked after by his sister. He had had several falls, but refused to get a wheelchair. I went so that his sister could take a badly needed vacation, and when I arrived I suggested again that he should get a wheelchair. "I would rather be dead than sit in a wheelchair", said my cousin. "Fritz", I said, "Do you remember a man called Roosevelt?" He looked at me. I continued: "If a wheelchair was good enough for him, then it is also good enough for you." "I don't want to be sitting idly in a wheelchair", said Fritz. "Was Roosevelt idle in his wheelchair?" I asked.

The next day I bought a wheelchair. "I don't want that thing in my room", said Fritz. "That's all right", I said, "I have invited it to live in my room." As we got ready to go out, I said: "You don't have to sit in it. Just take it along and we will push it to the park." Then, when we were ready to leave the park again, I suggested: "Sit in the wheelchair now, Fritz; you have walked enough. I'll give you a ride." And when we arrived home, Fritz said: "It's a good thing to have a wheelchair."

After my cousin died, I had another opportunity to introduce someone to a wheelchair. Mrs. Peters was an elderly widow, a refugee from Germany, who lived in a 2-roomed flat in a suburb of New York. She taught bridge, and sub-let one of her rooms to me. Mrs. Peters was handicapped; she wore a caliper on one leg, and could not get out at all. "Why don't you get a wheelchair", I asked her. "I have no space for it", she said, "And I couldn't let my pupils see me in a wheelchair — impossible." "The wheelchair is invited to stay in my room", I said, and brought one in the next day. I took her for walks in my free time, and sometimes her sister would take her out. One day Mrs. Peters confided in me: "I much prefer it when you take me out. When my sister does it, she makes me get out of the wheelchair at every street crossing. She says she cannot get it across with me sitting in it."

———

The years that followed were very difficult for me. In 1959, while on holiday in World Fellowship, I had what the doctor called a light stroke, and though I recovered after 2 - 3 months, I didn't feel well. They nursed me at WFS, and I stayed there to convalesce. That same winter saw Willard Uphaus' trial. He was found guilty of Contempt of Court by a 5 to 4 majority of the jury, and for us, his friends and supporters, this was a very upsetting time, but also exciting and invigorating as we became involved in the struggle for justice and human rights (*see Chapter 14 for a fuller account of his trial*).

Then in 1960 I suffered many falls and problems of balance, double vision and so on. My eye doctor found nothing wrong with my eyes and sent me to a neurologist. The neurologist put me into a hospital for observation and tests. These were very painful; the doctor suspected a brain tumour or a leaking blood vessel.

Then my spine started to get more and more troublesome, and as I had lost some disks and had some damaged vertebrae, I had to be put in a so-called tailor brace. For some months I had been wearing an orthopaedic corset to support my spine, then a higher one, and now it was to be a large steel brace, mounted on to an old-fashioned corset. It looked pretty awful and heavy, but the doctor was nice about it, and friendly. "Regard it as a good friend", he said, "It will help you to carry your back." And then he asked: "Have you somebody at home who will help you to put it on every morning?" "No", I said, "I live alone, in a furnished room. Show me exactly how to do it."

And then, after putting me in it, he asked: "Shall I wrap it up for you to carry it home?" "Oh no!" I said, "I will have to get used to it. I'd better start right now to wear it." It was 10.00 o'clock when I left the hospital, a cold, wet, autumn day. What now? Where shall I go? I walked down the stairs to the underground train. 'I will not go home', I thought, 'At home there would be the temptation to take it off.' I went to a museum in town. Then I had lunch in town. I wanted to stay away from 'home'. I had to get used to this very uncomfortable brace, and once at home I would take it off. So after lunch I went to a movie. It was a very long movie. At 6.00 pm I went home. 'I have managed to keep it on for over eight hours', I told myself, 'Now I can take it off.' But poor me! The zipper was broken. I could not get out of it. I had to sleep in it all night. The next morning I travelled back to the hospital in my brace.

It was not so easy to learn to live with the brace. I had been instructed how to manage to sit down on a chair, how to get up from the chair, how to get something out of the fridge, how to pick something up from the floor, how to cross the road. There was so much that 'you must never do', and when I finally asked: "How long will I have to wear it?" the doctor's answer was: "The day before you die you may take it off." It seemed that I was stuck; stuck in the brace. But I was determined to lead as normal a life as possible.

Well, I had to make some basic changes in my life. Working with children was out! Nursing sick people was out! I had to think of a sitting profession. I had to retrain. But how, and for what, at the age of 59? I was advised to learn re-touching and colouring of photographs. I enrolled in a big photographic school in New York for a 6-month course, after which I received a diploma as 'Colourist & Retoucher of Photographs', and a second one for airbrush work.

The school's Employment Office was to find me a job. Full of expectation I went for an interview. The employer liked my samples of work. When he said: "You start Monday 8.00 am" I asked to see the room where I would work. He took me there and introduced me to Rosa. She would tell me all about my job. She said: "I have been here 15 years. The first weeks I found it very hard, my back ached. But I got used to it. You see that big ladder over there, honey? You will climb up to the top." 'I will not', I thought. "And you work as far as you can reach out with your arm." 'I am not allowed to lift my arms higher than my shoulders', I thought. Rosa, in her joy to get a new helper, continued: "Then you move your ladder on. And that you keep on doing all day long, up and down the ladder; it becomes almost automatic." 'Not with me', that I knew. I was in that big brace. I had dizzy spells. I had falls. I was re-educated for a sitting occupation.

When I told the Employment Office that I could not accept this job, the secretary said: "Don't you at least want to try it for a fortnight?" And because I refused, they would not offer me any job at all. They took me off their list. So here I was in my big brace, with no job. What could I do? Finally I found a job with an establishment dealing in coloured photos which allowed people to work at home. Every day at noon I had to collect the work, two to three dozen black and white photos to colour. I worked from the minute I arrived home until 3.00 or 4.00 am. Then at 12.00 I delivered these photos and collected the new batch to be ready for the next day.

This was very difficult work, paid at piece-work rates, and I made about $2 - $3 a week, with which I had to pay my fares as well as the material to do the job. After some weeks I gave it up — and as so often in my life, good luck was with me. After wearing the brace for ten years, I had my first heart attack. I took the brace and threw it out of the window, as I was sure that its constriction had been the cause of the attack. First, though, I had another spell in Australia — with the brace.

CHAPTER 7

LIFE MOVES ON

IN 1963 I REVISITED AUSTRALIA for the first time since leaving in
1953. My friend Margaret and her daughter Robin met me at the airport, but Robin was no longer a little girl. Still, it was like coming home:
we felt as if we had never been separated, nor as if ten years had elapsed,
though I was now in the big steel brace which restricted me in many ways.
In the car I had to be propped up with cushions on both sides so that I
wouldn't tip over; my balance was very poor, but I was very happy to be
back.

Robin now drove her own car and we did quite a lot of sightseeing.
One day she took me to Bellrieve, a small island reached by ferry, and I
fell in love with it. The next morning I decided to take a packed lunch
and go to Bellrieve by myself for some sketching and painting. I took the
ferry across and started to walk around the island. Each time I stopped,
I thought I saw a nicer place a little further along. I walked along the
shore. There was nobody else - just nature and I. In front of me the deep
blue ocean and the endless beach. Over me the cloudless blue sky. And
behind me private villas in large park-like gardens.

Finally I started to paint. I did not have to watch the time, I had the
whole day, and when I paint I get so involved that nothing else exists,
nothing else matters. Today I felt like being absorbed by nature, like being
a part of nature. I seemed to be breathing and swaying in the rhythm of
nature. I felt in harmony with the nature around me, and my picture
seemed to be the echo of what I felt. It was a joyous, a colourful, a har-
monious picture.

I was still painting when all of a sudden a strong wind arose, a very
strong wind. I looked up at the sky: big black clouds! And now, the first

large drops of rain! Then thunder and lightning followed, and now it was pouring, pouring down like out of buckets. My easel had been blown over, my canvas lay in the sand, face down, my paints were scattered all over the sand. I, in a thin summer dress, was dripping wet. I tried to gather up my tubes of paint, my paint brushes and everything else, and then, as I lifted up my face, in front of me, like out of the earth - or rather like down from heaven - she stood: an elderly lady, tall and erect in a blue macintosh and with an open umbrella. Over her arm a second macintosh and a second umbrella. She pointed up to the hill. She said: "I live up there on that hill. I saw you from my window. I came to get you."

We walked up to her house in pouring rain and lightning. As we entered the house, her sister helped us to take off our wet raincoats. They brought me a wool blanket. They asked me to take off my wet clothes, so that they could get them dry for me. But I said: "I don't know if I can do that, I must catch the afternoon ferry. My friends in Hobart expect me to be back in time for dinner." "Who are your friends?" they asked. I told them. "Oh! Margaret! We know her very well. We can call her up. We will tell her that you are here with us and that she does not need to worry. We will take you to a later ferry after the storm is over."

They dried my clothes, they gave me a lovely dinner and later took me to the evening ferry. How I wished that I could see them again. Well, soon my wish was fulfilled. The next Sunday I went to the Meeting for Worship in the Quaker Meeting House, and there they were. I had not known that they were Quakers — and it was then that I decided I wanted to spend the last ten years of my life in Hobart, Tasmania.

———

Good friends of mine, Vivienne and Paul, had invited me to visit them in their new house in Melbourne, and Paul met me at the airport. The weather was bad, cold and wet, and it was a long drive to their new house, a beautiful house with every conceivable modern comfort. They showed me all over the new house. Then Vivienne asked me: "Ilse, would you like to have a cup of tea?" "I would love it", I said. Vivienne put on the kettle, and then she said: "Of course, you have had your dinner on the plane, haven't you?" My answer: "If you would have asked me that four weeks ago, I would have said 'Yes, thank you' but now I must say 'No', as I have just promised Margaret, when I left her, that I would always be honest, and that I would never use so-called white lies."

Vivienne was quite stunned: "You have not had your dinner on the plane? That's awful. I have nothing that I could give you. We had our dinner at 5.00 o'clock." I replied: "I am sure that you have some bread and butter. That will be fine." We had a long discussion on honesty in daily life. Said Vivienne: "You cannot always be honest; you have to abide by the general customs of the society in which you live. You cannot embarrass your friends." I said: "Let's be honest for the next three days. Let's call it the Quaker Game."

Being honest is one of the basic commitments for Quakers, I explained. Also when the phone rings, and you ask one of your children to answer the phone for you, then do not whisper: 'Say I am not here.' "But I might not want to talk", said Vivienne. "Jean can just say: 'Can I give mother a message?'" "But I might just be in the bathroom", said Vivienne. "Jean can say: 'Mother is in the bathroom. Can she call you back?' Be honest with your children also." For three whole days we did play the 'Quaker Game'. Also with friends and neighbours. And when I left, Vivienne said: "You know, Ilse, after all it's not such a bad idea. It makes life simpler, easier. You don't have to first think what's best to say. You just say it!"

———

After three happy days with this family in Melbourne, I went on to Sydney to visit my brother and sister-in-law, and several other friends. After that, I had to think of going back to America, but I had never been to New Zealand, and as this wasn't a big detour, I decided to go back that way. I had intended to stop over for one week, but the weather was very unfavourable: cold and rainy. After a few wet days in Christchurch, followed by a couple more in the North Island, I took off again from Auckland and the next stop was going to be Fiji.

I boarded the plane, and found that my neighbour was a tall black man with a handsome profile, which suggested that he was of Indian descent. He was dressed in a blue wool sweater with turtle neck and an English tweed jacket over it. Soon after we were in the air, dinner was served. As the stewardess put his dinner tray in front of him, a steak dinner, he shrank away from it. "Are you a vegetarian?" I asked him. "You can have it! Take, take", he said. I took the plate out of his sight, and rang my bell for the stewardess. He got a vegetarian dinner. In broken English he thanked me: "Very kind of you. Thank you, thank you", he said. Then he held up his cutlery, which was rolled up in a paper serviette. "What's that?" he asked. "That's your fork and knife and spoons",

I explained. Now he held up his fingers and said: "At home, in my house, we use natural tools - much easier."

After a while we were handed landing cards. Seeing that he had a pen, I asked him to lend it to me. His response was: "You not have pen but you can write. I have pen but I not can write. I give you pen, you write for me." While filling out his card I had to ask him all kinds of personal questions. And when after three hours we landed at Nandi Airport we were already friends. He was a small farmer in a small village near Sufa. He had been in New Zealand for three months as a guest worker, cutting trees in the forest. At home he had a wife and four children, and three children from his first wife. He invited me to his house. He told me that I would be the first white person to visit them. "Best thing you come right with me", he said. "No", I said, "No. You have been away from home for three months. You cannot come home now with a strange woman. Your wife would not like that."

But I promised to come within a week, and he explained how to get there: "Very easy", he said, "In Nandi you take big bus - only 7 or 8 hours - then in Sufa you take little bus - only 30 minutes. On little bus the driver, my brother, he show you my house." Some days later I stood with my large suitcase at what I hoped was the bus stop. There was no shelter, no bench, but it was sunny and very hot. I had been told: "The bus service is once a day. The bus passes by between 8.00 and 9.00 o'clock. You must hail it." Well, here I stood. After a long wait a taxi stopped. The driver offered to take me for a ride. I did not want to be taken 'for a ride'. But he explained that he had to pick up three people in the next village and take them to Sufa, and that I could share the taxi with them, and he would not charge me more than I would pay on the bus. I went with him. It turned out to be a most enjoyable day, a combination of sightseeing and transportation, an unforgettable trip. We were: a young couple, a middle aged woman, our young driver and I. We were of four different nationalities, but like one happy family. In the middle of the day we had dinner in a nice restaurant all together.

In the late afternoon we arrived at Sufa, where I checked in to a hotel. Sufa is a resort. The next morning found me in a swimming pool, and in the afternoon I was on my way to the bus terminal to find the 'Little Bus' that was to take me to my friend's village in thirty minutes. And what a beautiful ride that was! When my 'Stop' came, the driver told me: "Walk straight on through that valley on that little footpath and you get there." Yes, I got there. The path was not cemented, not hard earth either. Mud steps led up to my friend's small cottage. There he was standing on the porch in his mini bathing trunks. He was busy, clipping his son's hair, but happy to see me. The whole family gave me a warm welcome. His two little girls aged 10 and 11 learned English in school. They brought out their 'English Readers'. I let them read to me; I read to them. I helped them with their school work. But later, when I asked at what time I had to leave to catch my bus back to Sufa, they all seemed disappointed. They wanted me to stay for the night. I left, but promised to return the next day and stay for the night.

And the next day I was greeted by the two little girls with their English books tucked under their arms. They were waiting for me right at the bus stop, where I got off. The same evening we had the house full of visitors. My host, who was the Chief of the village, had asked everybody to come and meet me, me the white American visitor. They all sat on the floor in the living room, and I told them about America, and American children. And then I answered questions, a lot of questions, and it was a very happy meeting. When all the villagers had left again, my host said; "You sleep in my parents house. Their is house bigger. There you have room for yourself." What he had meant was that I would have a bed for myself. The second bed in that room was shared by his mother and her seventeen-year-old granddaughter, who apparently had given up her bed for me.

My host's family was of Indian Hindu descent. His parents did not speak English but they and I got on very well without a spoken language. They were delighted when I, the stranger, greeted them at our first meeting in the Indian way, bowing my head and holding my hands in front of me with my palms together. A bond was made between us right then.

The first night, when bedtime came, the granddaughter showed me my bed. I said that I would like to go to the toilet first. I knew that it was a little outhouse in the meadows. To get there you had to walk down a small trail, then cross a stream. There was just a wooden plank put across the stream. Of course there were no lanterns of any kind. I thought the granddaughter would escort me with a torch, but no. She said: "Just a minute", and then the grandmother came to the bedroom door. "Come", she said, and turned around and I followed her. She walked ahead of me, in her beautiful majestic way. She walked out of the house but not towards the meadow and the outhouse. She stayed close to the house. She walked around the house. The house stood on a hill, overlooking the village. All of a sudden she stopped. I looked at her. "Here", she said, "Here." And the far outreaching swing of her arm seemed to say: 'All this wide space is yours.'

Back in the bedroom, I realised that I was expected to lie on top of the bedspread with my dress on. That meant I had to sleep with my big steel brace. After some minutes I felt something warm touching me. The grandmother and granddaughter had covered me with a pre-warmed blanket. They were tucking it in so gently and caringly.

In the morning the granddaughter asked me: "Would you like to have a bath?" "Oh yes", I said, "That would be lovely." "Come with me", she said. We walked out of the house and into the kitchen, a small one-room building. My escort opened the window: "Now hold your arms outside the window." She filled a dish with clean water from a bucket and poured it over my hands. That was my bath. Later I saw the whole family walk down to the river, all in bathing suits, towels over their shoulders, soap in their hands. I realised that they did not want me to be embarrassed, me the white stranger.

We had our dinner in the grandparents' house, in their living room. The whole family sat on the floor, their legs crossed in front of them, their backs towards the wall. They held their wooden bowls between their legs, but grandmother and I sat at a regular table, which was covered with a white tablecloth, and we had chinaware dinner plates. In the middle of the table was the dish with the dinner: cooked rice with cooked vegetables with a vegetable gravy on top. There was a serving spoon. But we had neither fork nor spoon, only a small pancake-like something to eat with. Grandmother did it so graciously without dropping even one kernel of rice. I felt very clumsy. I found it impossible to eat rice and gravy without fork or spoon. Hoping that nobody would notice it, I took possession of the serving spoon. The next day, at dinner, there was a spoon lying next to my dinner plate and a spoon lying next to grandmother's dinner plate. 'That is hospitality, real hospitality', I thought.

On Sunday I went to church with Grace, the granddaughter. There were no benches; everybody sat on the floor. I, with my big steel brace, sat in the back on a window sill. After the service Grace was eager to have me meet the Missionary. We found her outside the church, surrounded by a cluster of Fijian children. Each child in turn handed his or her little notebook, to get a little silver star pasted into it. Each child was praised for 'having been to church'. As Grace introduced me to her, the Missionary asked her: "Why haven't you been in church last Sunday?" "I had to help my grandmother at home", said Grace. The friendly smile changed to an angry look: "That's no excuse!" she said. As we walked away, Grace said to me: "Why should it be bad to help my grandmother, when she needs my help at home? I will help her when she asks me to."

That visit in Fiji in the little village where I was the only white person, and the hospitality, tact and kindness of my black host and his family, was amongst the high points in my life. Many white people can learn a lot from the black people, when you meet them in their accustomed environment, in their own homes, where they feel secure, and are the hosts. You get the right picture of them. Unfortunately very often we only meet people from other races or colours when they are uprooted, having come as refugees, unsettled, insecure, and so we get a very wrong picture of them.

———

On returning to New York, I lived in small furnished rooms without cooking facilities, but I still painted. I went to the art studio of Harry Schulberg, whose pupil I had been about eight years before, and also here I met with human warmth and friendliness, and was very touched. The day I walked into Harry's studio, I told him: "Harry, I came to tell you that unfortunately I cannot come any more. You see, I am in a big steel brace now. I cannot stand in front of an easel. I am not allowed to lift my arm higher than my shoulder, and I'm sorry but I have to quit painting." Harry said: "Ilse, don't let the brace worry you. I will make it possible for you to paint. I will find a chair on which you can sit comfortably. I will put the easel down to the right height for you — and forget about money. As long as you're not working, you don't have to pay to come here. I expect you to be in next Saturday as usual." I kept on going to Harry, and I kept on exhibiting my paintings in Greenwich Village twice a year as I had done before, in the big open-air exhibition which is held there. I have always found that artists are very friendly, and there is a nice warm atmosphere amongst them. It is taken for granted that artists will help each other, and I was very happy to belong to them again.

———

As the arthritis in my spine was getting worse and worse, I decided to go to a place in Italy which specialised in mud-bath cures. Monte Grotto was a small village right in the country. There were also some German patients there who couldn't talk any Italian, so as a side job I acted as interpreter. I also wrote some German business letters for the hotel manager, who couldn't write German. The cure consisted of mud packs; they had their own springs there. The hot mud came right out of the earth, and the treatment was quite tiresome and painful, but very effective. When on the first day they suggested giving me the mud packs and mineral bath between 2.00 and 3.00 in the morning, I wasn't happy about it, but they told me that I should try it. I might like it, because I could go right back to bed afterwards, and they would give me my massage in bed, and then I would drop off to sleep and really have some hours of good relaxing sleep.

After trying it for one or two nights, I found it a very good idea. I could sleep longer in the morning, was brought my breakfast late into the room, and didn't have the day spoilt with treatment. I was free to do what I wished. They had told me at the start that the cure would only be of benefit if one took it for four years in succession, but I found that after the cure I got through the rest of the year with relatively little pain. When it did get worse, it was time to go back for the next cure. I did that in the years 1964 to 1967, and every time I went down to Florence or to Rome afterwards.

In Rome I always stayed with the nuns in the cloister. They had accommodation for about 30 tourists, and one was very well cared for there. I always had the same room looking down on the wall of St. Peter's, and it was basically furnished. The meals were simple but excellent. One sat ten at a long table, and the conversation went happily in four or five different languages. There were always interesting people there: African nuns, people from all over the world, and the Librarian of St Peter's was a permanent resident there. Several times I stayed there for four or six weeks.

Then the time came when I wanted to go to Australia for good, so I told my sister. "Why?" she said. "Because I want to spend the last 10 years of my life in Australia, and the last 10 years are starting now. I don't want them to be cut short." My sister and my brother didn't want me to go. They wanted the family to stay together, but I was determined to go. It was quite a struggle, and as I lived under a lot of stress at that time, and in a state of depression, I felt I would need a lot of inner strength and discipline to fight off the depression, make a break with New York, and go to Australia for good.

What did I do? I started to undertake what I myself called 'my treatment'. It was a very cruel treatment, but I stuck it out. Every day, in my little furnished room, in the afternoon, I pulled down my curtains, put on the radio so that the neighbours shouldn't hear what was going on,

110

and then I got undressed, lay flat on my stomach on a big table, and beat myself. I beat myself with a leather strap, then stood in front of the mirror to see if I had blue streaks on my back, and if I didn't think I had beaten myself enough, I would go on. I did this every day, and it became an addiction. Soon I began doing it twice a day, in the morning and in the afternoon, and when I took a walk in the street, I couldn't wait to get home again for my 'treatment'. This went on for about two or three months.

I intended to go to Australia by freighter, because I had a lot of big baggage to take with me. I asked my doctor if I could go to Australia by boat and he said: "No." ""Why not?" I asked. "Because if you fall and break a bone, that would be the end of you." "Doctor", I said, "Don't I have the same right to break bones like everyone else?" "No", he said, "Other people's bones will mend, but your bones will not mend because you have osteoporosis." After the doctor said I couldn't go by freighter, I thought I'd try out how I liked it, and instead of going straight to Australia, I would first take a short trip, of 11 days instead of 35 days. I took a freighter to Holland. The sea was very rough, and the captain told us that on the last trip, three weeks earlier, one person broke her nose, another a wrist and a third one a hip.

When the going got really very rough, I played sea-sick and stayed in my berth for three days, so as not to fall. Of course, because I told them that I was sea-sick, they only gave me tea and rusks to eat, a strict diet. The Captain was a friendly young man, but fond of drinking, and every evening he was really drunk. My cabin companion, a very nice woman, felt sorry for him, and wanted to take care of him, but didn't want to do so by herself, so she asked me to help her. Every evening, when we thought that it was bed-time for the Captain, we went to his apartment, a nice suite of bedroom and living room, and the two of us got him undressed and into bed.

Some months later I was really off to Australia on another freighter. We started our trip in New York, and our first port of call was Charlotte in the South. As soon as I got on board, I realised that there wasn't one chair on the boat in which I could sit with my steel brace, not easy chairs or upholstered chairs, and the deck chairs were of canvas in which I couldn't sit either, so when we stopped in Charlotte for three hours, I left the boat and went into a department store to buy a chair. I tried out about 15 different chairs, and finally bought a rocking chair. It had a steel frame and could be folded like a garden chair. When I returned to the boat, there was much amusement amongst my companions. They all laughed and said: "Don't you think the boat will rock enough without the rocking chair?" When we got out into the open ocean, though, I found I was much better off in my rocking chair than anybody else in their regular deck chairs. My chair rocked in rhythm with the sea.

I always left the chair on deck, and in the evening put it behind one of the big sand boxes so as not to have to carry it down to my cabin, but one morning when I came up on deck, the rocking chair was gone. That was a shock for me. Where was the rocking chair? I really needed it badly, and I couldn't understand how it could have fallen off. It was really impossible to fall off, I thought. The Deck Steward didn't see it anywhere. We went all over the boat, and all the 11 passengers helped me to look for it, but it wasn't anywhere. In desperation we went up to the bridge to see the Captain. He gave us permission to go into the crew's cabins, and in the cabin of the 1st Officer we found the rocking chair. The Captain told me not to leave it on deck any more because he didn't want the 1st Officer to take naps during the night in my chair instead of standing on the bridge.

The trip to Sydney takes 35 days, a long time, and after a while it gets quite monotonous; you start longing to see a tree or a flower, or at least some grass. One gets really tired of seeing only water, water, water, and it really became an attraction when someone on the other side of the boat spotted a bird. We all rushed over to see that bird, or a fish, or a piece of driftwood, or a whale in front of the boat. We also had a so-called swimming pool on the boat. It was really an old tank filled with ocean water, but on rough days we were advised not to use the 'pool' because of the possibility of being thrown out into the ocean.

Our accommodation was excellent. The cabin was really a large room with good furniture: a real bed, wardrobe, settee, low table and easy chairs. Meals were served in the dining room, which was furnished like in a private villa, with a big French door opening to the living room, where coffee was served after meals. We also had our own baker on board, which meant fresh rolls for breakfast every morning and home-baked cakes for afternoon tea. The meals were excellent and we were really treated royally.

After a brief stay in Sydney I went on to Hobart, where I was to become a resident in Strathaven Lodge, an old-age home. Strathaven Lodge was run by the Methodist Church, and was a very friendly place. Its location was beautiful, about half an hour outside Hobart, right in the country and near to a bay. There were 60 residents, each with their own

112

room and furniture, and their own garden in front - except me. I didn't want a garden, since I couldn't do any gardening in my big brace, but my neighbours always saw to it that I had fresh flowers in my room.

We, the twenty residents of the so called New Wing in the home, had a small pantry with a small fridge for our personal use. The home supplied us with milk, bread, butter and jam, and we could put our own snacks in it. One of the ladies put in whole cream pies and big jars with soup. That took up too much space, so the Matron put a note outside on the door of the fridge: 'Please be aware that this fridge is for 20 people. You are only entitled to a twentieth part of the space available.' This note had no effect. The large cream pies continued to fill up the fridge. And now I hung up a note inside the fridge. It actually jumped into your face as soon as you opened the fridge: 'Everybody is invited to help himself to anything that is in this community chest'. The problem was solved. The big pies were not put in any more. Their owner told me later that she did not want to share them with anybody.

———

It was not until 1967 that I officially joined the Religious Society of Friends. People have often asked me how I came to the Quakers. What made me decide to join them? I must say that it wasn't a sudden decision, and it wasn't that I was looking for a church group because I wasn't satisfied with the group to which I belonged before. No. All my life I considered myself as a German citizen of Jewish religion, but not practising any religion. I regarded myself as a free thinker. And, as I said before, it wasn't a sudden decision to join the Quakers. No, I just grew into that movement, or into that way of thinking.

I think I was very lucky that already in the beginning of my life, already as a small child, I had a social conscience. I was born into a so-called 'good family', that meant into the so-called upper middle class, but strangely enough I never felt very comfortable belonging to that class. Already as a child I resented behaving like a so-called 'better class' person. Then when I started to have a profession I felt very happy and very comfortable working in homes for poor children, in homes in the slums of New York, in homes for so-called 'problem children' who were in trouble with the law. As I said, I always had a social conscience.

As a school child at the beginning of the First World War I was very impressed by the Quakers who were conscientious objectors, who refused to go into the war and shoot people, people who had never done anything to them, soldiers who were supposed to be their enemies, but whom they had never met face to face. Then in Hitler's time again I realised that the Quakers did a lot of good work helping people, distressed people, people who were in dire need of help. They didn't only help their own people. They helped everybody, regardless of race or religion. They were tolerant.

My first personal meeting with Quakers was in 1949 when I visited Australia for the first time. I met Margaret Wilkinson and her family and in her house I met many Quakers. I found the Quakers very friendly, very outgoing, and I felt very much at home with them. It was in the year 1949 that I first started to go to Quaker Meetings in Sydney. At that time I lived in my brother's house with my brother and his wife and when I asked his wife to look up in the telephone book the address of the Sydney Quaker House she said to me: "Yes, I have found it. But you cannot go there." "Why not?" I said. "Oh", she said,"it's in a very bad district of the town, in a very poor district. You cannot walk there." Of course I did go there, and I started to go to Quaker Meetings, and I started to be, you could say, an Attender. I was an Attender for many, many years.

———

In July 1968 I got the news that my youngest brother was critically ill in Switzerland, and next day I was on my way to see him. I flew to Zurich, and from there to Davos, where my brother was. I stayed with him for about four weeks, then, as soon as he was able to be moved, I took him by plane back to New York. When we arrived, my sister asked me if I could take the other brother on vacation, because the family with whom he lived in New York had gone on vacation themselves for four or five weeks. I went with this brother to Monhagan Island, the beautiful little artists' island 14 miles off shore in the Atlantic.

We had spent several vacations there and had always liked it very much. After five weeks I brought him back, and found my sister was in the hospital with a broken hip. That meant I had to stay on in New York and take care of her for two weeks after she was released from hospital. By that time I was ready to go back home, but when I called up my good friend in Hobart and told her that I would be coming back, she said: "Ilse, after all you went through during the last two months with your two brothers and your sister, and all that stress, worry and work, I advise you not to come back straight away. Go to Pendle Hill, the American Quaker Study Centre, at least for a weekend to rest before you come back."

114

On Friday I went up to Pendle Hill for what I thought would be a weekend. I liked Pendle Hill very much, and as I noticed on the board that a new semester was starting on Monday, I enrolled as a student for that semester. While I was the youngest resident in the old age home in Hobart, here in Pendle Hill as a student I was the oldest in a group of 45. I enjoyed it very much. It was a beautiful feeling, all of a sudden at the age of 66, to be a student again amongst all the young people. I really got a new lease of life there. I started to be very active, did a lot of writing encouraged by my counsellor, to whom I had read some of my writing, to keep on writing and really write a journal. I even wrote a term paper which I read to the whole faculty at the end of the semester.

Sokei and Masako were amongst the first students whom I met. I was horror-stricken when I realised that I harboured a hidden prejudice against them. Why? Because they were Japanese, and a Japanese soldier had killed a woman with his bayonet, and the woman happened to be my brother's wife. That was 23 years ago. I had never met Japanese people. Now I was face to face with them and also face to face with my own prejudice - and I realised that I also still had a resentment against the Germans. How could I get rid of my resentment against the Japanese? I had to do something about it. I went and knocked on Sokei's door. I told him my story. He listened quietly. When I was finished, he said two words: "I understand". Then we shook hands. The grey wall disappeared. The wall which had been there for so many years was no more, and out of its rubble a new friendship grew.

———

In December 1968 I sadly said goodbye to Pendle Hill and went back to Hobart, and Strathaven, only now I didn't feel so happy there any more. While I had been away nine months, we had, it seemed, grown in opposite directions. I had become younger again, more active. Strathaven had become older. When I first joined as a resident, the admission age was 62. Now the rules had been changed and no new residents were admitted under 80, so it was slowly becoming something like a nursing home.

Also I still felt this resentment against the Germans, which even went so far that I didn't buy anything which carried a tag saying that it was 'Made in Germany'. I had had this since Hitler's time and I really felt that now, being a Quaker, it wasn't right to harbour resentment against anybody. I was thinking about how I could get rid of that resentment; here I was, belonging to the Quakers, and still harbouring resentment against other people.   That wouldn't do. So in the year 1970 I decided that I had to do something to rid myself of it. I decided to take a year's leave of absence from Strathaven, go to England, meet English Quakers and then go to Germany and meet German Quakers. I regarded German Quakers as less 'German' and more as a 'world family', and I thought that they would create a 'bridge' for me to the German people.

CHAPTER 8

A PILGRIMAGE

AT THE BEGINNING OF 1970 I started my pilgrimage. I visited all the Quaker Centres and Guest Houses in England: Old Jordans, Charney Manor and so on, and after six months I was ready to go to Germany. The last two weeks I spent again in Claridge House, and here on my very last day in England, an old lady asked if I would do her a favour. She told me that many, many years ago she had been in Germany in a place called the *Freundshaftsheim* on her honeymoon. She wanted me to go and see if this place still existed, though she didn't have any address. All she knew was that it was the *Freundshaftsheim* in Bückeburg. And so the next day I started my pilgrimage to Germany and my first stop was going to be Bückeburg. I arrived in Bückeburg at noon. Now I was on German soil — for the first time after 37 years. It was a beautiful autumn day. The sky was blue, the sun was shining. Here I was standing with my big trunk. What next?

I took my trunk to the baggage-room and then asked the attendant if he knew of a place called *Freundschaftsheim*. He did. "Where is it?" I asked. "Up there, on that hill." "What bus can I take?" "Bus", he said, "Bus? There is no bus in Bückeburg." "Which tram goes up there?" "Tram? We don't have any trams here." He looked me over and then said: "I see you have good strong walking shoes; you can walk." "How long will it take me?" "About one hour, if you walk with determination."

I had a hearty meal at the station restaurant; it felt strange to sit there in my home-country and yet to be a foreigner. Then I started my walk up the hill. After about forty-five minutes I came to a cross-road, and wondered which way to take. There was a filling station there, and the woman in charge was quite friendly. We had a nice chat. Then, all of a sudden, she pointed to a negro across the street. She told me to just follow him, as he was on his way to the *Freundschaftsheim* also. And so I did.

When I arrived, I walked into the office and was received by a young Indian in her colourful sari. To my dismay she explained that they did not accommodate 'tourists'. They were an educational enterprise now for training foreign students in closed groups. While this lady was talking to me a minister came in, apparently the director of the place. I told him why I had come. "Oh yes", he said to the Indian lady, "'Miss Karger can stay here for the weekend." "We have no vacant room", said the lady. The minister replied: "One of our staff members is away for the weekend." The lady: "But her sheets are on the bed." Minister: "You take them off and put clean ones on for Miss Karger." Then he invited me to have coffee with him in his private villa. There I met his wife and two young children, 2½ years old. After we had had coffee, I offered to take the children for a walk, to give the young mother some time to go on with her work (she had been busy with ironing when we dropped in). I was amazed that this young mother trusted me, a complete stranger, with two young children. Off I went with the big pram and one child holding on. After a long walk we returned happily. Then the minister contacted a Quaker family, the only Quaker family in Bückeburg. This Friend, Gerd Wieding, came over to meet me and so my first contact with the German Quakers was made.

The next day I was invited to join the students in a day's outing by bus. I was the only white person on this trip, the only Jewish person, the only American citizen, and the oldest one there, aged 68. We arrived in Hameln and were received by the mayor, and fêted by a beautiful afternoon tea party. In his speech, the mayor said that this year, like every year, he was very glad to be able to greet this party from four different continents. The leader of our group, the minister from Bückeburg, interrupted him and said: "Excuse me, sir. This year I am glad to tell you that we are representing five continents, because Miss Karger has just arrived from Australia." It was very strange for me, as a born German, to represent Australia in Hameln; I also represented America, as I was now an American citizen, and also the white race and the Jewish religion.

———

From there I went to Berlin, where I was the guest of another German Quaker, Gertrude Krause. I took a taxi from the station, and the route took us through the district in which I had grown up, and lived and worked for the first 30 years of my life. It was a strange feeling for me to see the names of the streets, and to pass the house where I had run my private nursery school. I had not been in Berlin for 37 years. Berlin had changed, and I also had changed. And there had been the war. Many houses were not there any more, including the house where I had lived with my parents for so many years. In its place there was nothing, just an empty lot.

Gertrude had arranged for me to meet another Quaker. When I met her at the *Kurfürstendamm*, she suggested a visit to the new *Hansaviertel*. "You'll be surprised", she said. "It's marvellous how they've rebuilt it. It's beautiful, like a new town. There are many beautiful things there." But I said: "If you don't mind, I'm not interested in the *Hansaviertel*, or the elegance of Berlin. I don't want to walk around in the beautiful *Tiergarten*. Couldn't we go to a small place where we can sit and just talk? I don't want to go sightseeing. It's not easy for me to be here in Berlin. I left Berlin under very difficult circumstances."

So we sat down in a coffee shop, and spent some hours there. Then she suggested that I might like to see the *Kaiser Wilhelm Gedächtniskirche*, the main church in Berlin at the end of the *Kurfürstendamm*. It had been badly bombed during the war, but they had left the roof of the church open as a memorial, and had added a new modern small chapel, right next to the church, and we went to this chapel. I was impressed by this simple, modern, unpretentious, beautiful chapel. A short service was held there every evening at 6.30, for just 20 minutes, and we attended this. It was a very touching service; the people who came were from all classes: workers came with their tool boxes, people from all walks of life and all professions, and I was really very impressed.

On my second day in Berlin, I looked through the telephone book for the address of a friend. Her two children had attended my nursery school, and the mother and I had become very good friends. I found her name and called her on the phone. "Are you Mrs. von Roy?" "Yes," she said. I said: "You might not remember me. I haven't been in Berlin for a long time." She said: "What is your name?" "Ilse." "Ilse?" she said, "Ilse! No! It's really you? Then my thoughts and prayers have not been in vain. You are still alive. Where are you?" "I am here in Berlin. May I visit you?" "Yes, yes, by all means. Please do come." I said: "How is your family?" "My family?" she said, "I am alone now. My two boys did not come back from the war. One died in a Russian prison camp and the other one fell defending Berlin at the end of the war. My husband is in a nursing home; he is mentally sick." The next day I went to visit her, and during the two weeks I stayed in Berlin, I visited her every other day.

119

After spending a week with Gertrude Krause, I took a room in a small guest house, bed and breakfast, in that street of Berlin where I had grown up. The first morning as I came into the dining room, I noticed a young Indian woman in a sari, sitting alone at a table. I approached her in English. She said that she was on a business trip, had to visit some firms in East Berlin which were her customers for fabrics. She did not speak German; I offered to be her interpreter. I spent the whole day with her in East Berlin, a very interesting and happy day, and in the afternoon we visited a Quaker couple in East Berlin, whom I had contacted by phone.

That evening, before returning to West Berlin, we went to a restaurant. But we had not much East German money left. My Indian friend was very hungry. I studied the menu card, and ordered one whole dinner for my friend. "And what for you?" the waiter asked. "Thank you, I will have just a glass of fresh water." "Why?" was his next question. "Because I have not enough money left." "I can bring you a cheese sandwich, or a salad." "No, thank you, I will be alright." He brought the dinner for my friend, and for me a bottle of water, a salad, and a cheese sandwich. "It's a present from our restaurant, you don't have to pay for it", he said. I had a long conversation with that waiter. He felt that young people like himself felt too 'restricted' because they could not travel outside the German Democratic Republic. In one of the fabric houses I talked to the manager's secretary. She felt very happy, she said, not to live in the snobbish West Berlin. "I have three children. The schools are much better here. And the sports. And the whole health system. I would not want my children to walk around the *Kurfürstendamm*", she said.

———

From Berlin I went on to Hanover, then to Frankfurt, Köln and Düsseldorf, and everywhere I was received with warmth and friendship, and felt as a Friend amongst Friends. It was a beautiful experience. In those Quaker houses, where I was given hospitality, I was really taken in to the family to share their family life with its joys and its problems. And strange as it may sound, I seemed to feel especially at home with those families who had problems. There was for instance Christine in Frankfurt. I arrived at her house at 10.00 o'clock on a cold winter morning. She introduced herself, then called her daughter: "Ingrid, this is Ilse, take her in and let her meet your friends." We walked into the dinning room. Around a large oak table six girls were having their tea. Ingrid walked around the table from one girl to the next and said: "This is my friend Susy, this is my friend Lotte", and so on, introducing each of her friends with a happy smile. They seemed to be a happy group, and yet they all had a handicap, including Ingrid herself: Downs Syndrome. They were aged between 23 and 26, and spent five days a week in Christine's house from 9.00 am. to 5.00 pm. Christine taught them housekeeping, cooking and cleaning, and in the afternoon handicrafts, sewing, knitting, and weaving. I spent two happy weeks with Christine and her friends.

From Frankfurt I went to Köln to see the Neighbourhood Centre, or *Nachbarschaftsheim*. This was started by a group of English Quakers who had gone there after the war to help rebuild the city. Hilda Loos, the director of the place, met me at the railway station and took me to a hotel which the Quakers had booked for me. The next morning, and every morning for the whole week, a car from the *Nachbarschaftsheim* called for me. I spent all day there, and loved every minute of it. I visited their nursery groups, attended their staff meetings, visited their old age centre, and I had all my meals with the staff. They also had 'The Open Door' for young people. It was a beautiful experience for me to see this wonderful place, where, under one roof, they cared for so many different needs.

Doris Roper, an English Quaker, and one of the original members of the group of English Quakers, had stayed on there as Secretary. While I was there, she celebrated her 25th anniversary of service. I will never forget that beautiful afternoon. She stood there, and after the city's Mayor had presented her with a gift, she timidly said: "How can I accept a present when I live here so happily? I love to be here, and to work here, so how can I accept a present for doing so?"

From Köln I went on to Düsseldorf, where I was again invited into a family with a handicapped child. When I arrived at their house at noon, a woman, apparently the cleaning lady, opened the door, and told me that Susan had just gone out to pick up her younger child from school, but would be home soon. She showed me into the sitting room. I sat down. A minute later a boy of maybe 10 appeared at the open door. He looked in, but disappeared again. He did that several times. I had noticed a box with building blocks. I sat down on the floor. I started to play with these blocks. The boy came to the door again, he came into the room, but very shy and careful, just for a minute, and then out he was again. "Come in", I said. He came in and went out again. He danced rather than walked. And every time he came in he stayed a fraction of a minute longer. And then I said: "I need your help. Help me to build a tower." And now he sat down on the floor opposite me, and together we built a tower; I had made a contact with Manuel, an autistic boy.

121

I had with me a booklet with the names of all the German Quakers, and was told to call them wherever I was, and try to visit them. Whilst in Düsseldorf I called up Cläre Stölting. I was told that she was an elderly Quaker who lived in a little town some way out of Düsseldorf, and who would surely be glad to meet me. When I called her up, she invited me for the next day, a Sunday. It was a long bus ride, 45 minutes, but finally I got to Lindorf, the little village where she lived. I got off the bus and walked down her street, and in the middle, between her house and the bus stop, she came to meet me — a lady without a hat, not really elderly, looking very friendly. She looked at me and said: "I think we two are seeking each other." That was her greeting.

Her next question was: "Are you Jewish?" I said: "Yes, I am." She said: "Oh, if I had known that, you wouldn't be in a hotel in Düsseldorf. You would be here in Lindorf, in my house. Now let's go and have some dinner." After we had had our dinner she said: "Now I'm going to take advantage of you. I am just translating an article from the English weekly Quaker journal, 'The Friend', for the German Quakers, and you can help me with it." So we worked together for some hours. The afternoon passed very quickly, and after three hours we felt as if we had known each other for many years. We were not strangers any more.

Then she took me to the bus stop and I went back to my hotel in Düsseldorf, but the next morning I called her up and said: "I would like to visit you once more. May I come out again to see you?" "Oh yes, yes. Do come." We spent that day together again, and then made an appointment to meet on the following day to visit an art gallery in Düsseldorf together.

Cläre and I met at 12.00 o'clock at the bus stop, and as it was pouring with rain, I suggested that we should have a cup of coffee before doing anything else. We sat there, in a very nice place, had coffee and cake, and a long, long chat. Finally Cläre looked at her watch and said: "Ilse, we cannot go to the art gallery any more. It is ten to five and it closes at 5.00 o'clock." So we went to my hotel for some hours instead, and then said goodbye to each other.

I then travelled some more around Germany, and in the middle of December I heard again from Cläre. I had written to her and suggested we might meet somewhere over Christmas. Cläre had replied that she had to stay in Lindorf because of an old sister-in-law whom she couldn't leave, but invited me to go there instead. However, I had just accepted an invitation to stay with Christine in Frankfurt, so I went to Cläre for a week over Christmas, and returned to Christine and her family for a further week.

———

Later, in the year 1971, I spent some weeks convalescing in Nelly Sachs House, a residential home for elderly Jewish people in Düsseldorf, located next to a beautiful, big, national park. At the time I was there, there were about 45 residents. The building was large and spacious and very comfortable and well furnished, but the atmosphere was tense, and felt as if a cold war was still going on between the Jewish residents and the Christian staff. The residents were old; some of them had left Germany in Hitler's time, and had lived as refugees in Africa or America, and at the end of the 1960's had returned to Germany to spend their old age in their homeland, as they thought. But of course Germany was not the same as it had been when they were children or young people. Their houses were not there any more. Their friends and relatives had gone, many in the Holocaust which they themselves had escaped, and they were not the same either. Now they lived in Nelly Sachs House, and felt old and lonely.

The staff were all middle-aged or youngish people. Some of them had been in the Hitler Youth as children. They had been fed with anti-semitism, of which they probably thought they had rid themselves now, but there still was no real warmth or understanding between the staff and the residents. To me it seemed that the poison of the bitter fruits of the aftermath of the devilish Hitler time was still in the air. The manager was a middle-aged Jewish man, who tried to rule by the power of a loud voice. Helped by his microphone and public address system, he yelled all through the house, but he was not able to get the staff and the residents any nearer to each other. The elderly residents in some ways provoked the staff by trying to order them around and command things of them, and the staff of course resented being ordered around, and showed their resentment by rude answers. It was very sad for me to witness all this.

The only bright spot in the whole place was the receptionist, a young conscientious objector who was doing alternative service. Instead of one year in the army he was allowed to work eighteen months in a social insti-tution, and for him that was Nelly Sachs House. He really was a nice, bright chap, friendly to everybody, and liked by everybody. I don't know what it is like now, but I feel that it takes more than two generations to heal those very deep wounds which were inflicted on the Germans in Hitler's time - not only to the Jewish people, but also those infected with the poison of anti-semitism which was fed to all the Christian children and young people in Hitler's time. Maybe it will take several generations to get over this, but hopefully Nelly Sachs House is a better place now than it was 20 years ago.

JLKA

'Who knows?'

CHAPTER 9

CLÄRE

THAT DAY IN DÜSSELDORF in 1970, when I was on my way to Cläre's house, and she met me in the street and greeted me with the words: "*Ich glaube, wir beide suchen einander*" (I think we two are seeking each other) was the start of our friendship. It was a very close friendship; "*Wir hatten uns gefunden*" (we really found each other) and it lasted until her death. It seemed that I reminded Cläre of her friend Daisy, whom she had lost only a few years earlier. Quite often she called me 'Daisy' by mistake. Daisy was short, dark haired, had big black eyes ('Like you, Ilse' said Cläre, 'And she was lively and active, like you').

In the Depression following the war, when her father's factory went bankrupt, Cläre decided that the family would have to sub-let their large house, and so she rented some rooms out to Daisy, a young English musician. Cläre herself helped to support the family by teaching foreign languages; she had studied at Oxford, and had a big love for England and the English people. England had almost become Cläre's second home, and her English was much better than mine. As we spent so much time together, I was always referred to as her English friend.

Cläre was already nearing 80 when we first met, but she was so active and alive, both physically and mentally. We shared in everything; there was nothing we did not do. We were never separated for longer than five or six weeks. We travelled, we attended Seminars and Retreats. I remember so well when we planned our first vacation together; we said: 'What do we expect of our summer vacation? Let's see - of course we want nice scenery, and good food, but that's not all. We also want mental and spiritual food'. We went to many different places together and had many different experiences: Autogen training, transcendental meditation, reflexology, pendulum divining, and many others. In one place we were the only guests who were not anthroposophists; in another we were the only Germans and had to talk nothing but French. Our experiences were always interesting, and always a lot of fun. We often behaved like little boys, climbing over fences and under barbed wire to take short cuts, and wading through streams.

One of our vacation places was Norway, quite an adventure. We had booked for two weeks into a very nice hotel in Ulvik, right on the Hardanger Fjord. Our room was in the annexe and had two doors - one door to the corridor of the annexe leading into the main house, and the other door leading straight out to the fjord. There were only a couple of metres between our door and the water, and very close to our room was the swimming pool - an open air pool which was filled with the fjord water. The first night I woke up at three o'clock in the morning, and ventured to go in my night dress to the swimming pool, climbed down the steep ladder and put my toe into the water. As I didn't find it too cold, I went swimming in that very nice pool the next morning.

That same afternoon Cläre went to the village and bought herself a bathing suit so that she also could go into the pool. At that time she was 84 and she didn't know how to swim, and the pool was deep, but I started to give Cläre swimming lessons, and she was most enthusiastic. We often got into our bathing suits after breakfast and took out one of the small rowing boats which belonged to the hotel. Cläre had never before been in a rowing boat, so I did the rowing, and Cläre did the steering. Usually we rowed over to a small island. It took us a little less than an hour to get there, and it was an idyllic spot. There was no house, no shelter, no human being to be seen at all, only bushes and berries and birds, and a heavenly quiet. I would pull the boat up a little bit. There was no tree or anything to tie up the boat, so I just pulled it up half out of the water, and we made ourselves comfortable. We lay there and read, or we just dreamed, or listened to the birds.

On day, when we were on the island, Cläre sat up and said: "Ilse, the boat is gone", and really there was no boat. Cläre got a bit panicky. "What shall we do? How can we get back home to the hotel?" I just said laughingly: "Oh, Cläre, that's nothing! We are just going to play Robinson Crusoe. We are here now on the island. We might find some nuts or berries to eat." Cläre asked: "How will they know in the hotel that we are marooned?" "At the evening meal, or even already at lunch time, they will miss us in the dining room, and they will contact the police and the police will maybe get a helicopter or boat and start looking for us. We will be found, I'm sure." Then, after some minutes, I decided to go and look for the boat, and found that the wind had driven it around behind the bay.

———

Cläre thought that I was the organiser of all our trips and travels, and to the casual observer I really was. I organised our movements, our travels and so on, but Cläre was the driving force with her enthusiasm. Findhorn, in the north of Scotland, was another one of our summer vacations in the summer of 1975. My nephew felt that I should go and have a look, but in his letter he wrote: "They are very fussy at Findhorn about whom they allow to come and visit as a paying guest, and if they should tell you 'No' when you put in your application, you have to answer them back that you will not take 'No' for an answer." He also told me that I must send a short autobiography, telling them what I have done in my life, what is my profession, why I want to visit. So that I did, and as an answer they sent me about six leaflets of literature about Findhorn, and in their letter they said 'Please study those leaflets thoroughly - really do read them through - not just leaf through them, and after reading all those leaflets, if you still want to come here, write to us.' I read the leaflets and I wrote back to them that I wanted to come.

Now they wrote to me: 'Bring working clothes with you, because we will make you work, and for the evening, bring one evening dress'. I went to Findhorn and took Cläre as a visiting guest. We arrived and took a taxi from the station. On the way, the taxi had to pass a public caravan site which didn't look very elegant; indeed, it looked pretty slummy, and as we drove into Findhorn we realised that it had as neighbours on one side this noisy big caravan site, and on the other side an army camp with a high wire fence around it, barbed wire on top, and two soldiers in full uniform with weapons. That didn't make us feel very happy, but once in Findhorn, the atmosphere changed completely.

We found Findhorn a very friendly place. It was a community of 120 residents who lived there permanently — ages from birth to 90. The residents worked eight hours a day for their keep. Most of them lived in their own caravans. Besides the 120 residents we were a group of 40 or 45 so-called paying visitors. We, the visitors, lived in very nice modern cottages. Every cottage had two double rooms, a living room, a separate dining room, a modern bathroom and a modern kitchen. That meant two couples could live in one cottage. The people in the cottages made their own breakfast, but everything was supplied by the community's kitchen, and in a very generous way. There in the kitchen we found bread, butter, milk, cheese, marmalade - everything was there. The other meals were taken in the main dining room in the main house. The food was excellent.

Our daily routine was as follows: by 7.00 o'clock in the morning you were supposed to have had your breakfast, you were supposed to have tidied up your cottage, washed your dishes, and made your beds. You were told that later in the morning somebody from the permanent staff would come around and see if your cottage was clean and tidy. Then at 7.15 you walked to the chapel for morning worship. It was a nice walk to the chapel and of course you had to leave your shoes or sandals outside. The service started with a short reading, and then there was quiet meditation for about half an hour. After that we were told what our work would be for the morning. Michael, a young permanent resident, was in charge of the so-called visitors. We sat in a circle in the lounge and awaited our daily work assignment: in the kitchen, in the house, the garden, the weaving shop, the printing shop and so on.

Before we started working, we stood together for what was called 'tuning in', a new and very interesting experience for me. As we stood in a circle, shoulder to shoulder, and held hands, and stood quietly there for some minutes together, I had the feeling that a strong electric current was going through all our bodies, and that after standing like this together, we were not six or eight individual people any more, but were united into one body, one family. From that minute on, it felt as if we had known each other for a long time, as if we belonged to each other. The atmosphere in which we then did our work was a very good one, a very friendly one, a very caring one, and this 'tuning in' was done every morning in the group with which we were going to work that day.

The first day I was assigned to the head gardener. He walked to a kind of shelter with me, where there were many empty flower pots; he told me that the pots needed a good scrubbing, and that was going to be my job for the morning. Strangely enough, I didn't feel any resentment because, instead of working in the garden, I had to be in that shelter and scrub empty flower pots. I was quite happy. Another day, I volunteered to work in the weaving shop, because I knew how to weave, how to operate a big loom, and I loved weaving. When the manager of the weaving shop walked with me to the shop, there was a big pile of wool lying in the middle of the shop, on the floor. Sue, the manager, said: "Today we are going to wind up the wool." She turned some chairs upside down on the table, and instead of being allowed to weave, I had to wind up wool all morning from 9.00 to 12.45, and strangely enough, again I didn't mind it because the atmosphere in the shop was such a friendly and cheerful one.

This was the thing we found in Findhorn. I had never anywhere in the world (and I have travelled a lot) found such a group of people, of all ages, who came from different parts of the world, people with different nationalities, and every one of them sparkling and friendly and happy all the time. We were there as visitors for two weeks, and we loved every minute of it. Yes, we were very happy there, but after two weeks we felt so exhausted that we needed a vacation from this vacation.

———

Another memorable vacation was spent at a small guest-house in Woodcote in Cornwall. We had been told to take the train to Lelant which lies between St. Erth and St. Ives, so we got off there and looked around. We were told that Woodcote was easy to reach in less than 10 minutes, and here we stood at the station with all our baggage. There was no shelter, not even a bench to sit on or a telephone. What could we do? I left Cläre standing there and went to find our guest-house. It really was a short walk, in a beautiful location with a beautiful garden. I walked up to the house and looked around. Nobody to be seen. I walked in and approached what was apparently one of the guests, and told her that we had just arrived, and needed someone to pick our bags up at the station. She said there was nobody around right now, but she could lend me some wheels to put under the suitcases. Then I saw a man standing near a car, and approached him. He turned out to be the owner of the guest-house, so I asked him to come down with his car and pick our baggage up. He said: "I'm sorry, I can't use the car just now. My family is sitting in it." Later it turned out that the 'family' were his four big dogs, who apparently lived in it, but nevertheless he himself came down and took our baggage up. The atmosphere at Woodcote was very good and friendly, the food was vegetarian, and we had the opportunity to make very nice day excursions by bus all over Cornwall, so it was a very good vacation for us. We were also introduced to spiritual healing, the interest and hobby of the owner of the guest-house.

One rainy, miserable day we decided to spend the afternoon shopping in St. Ives. We walked down to the little station at Lelant, which of course had no waiting room or bench to sit down on. There were already six people waiting and two prams, but we found out that the next train, due in ten minutes, would pass through our station but not stop.

According to the timetable we would have to wait 1½ hours. "We will stop that train when it comes in ten minutes", I said, "Why should we all stand here in the rain and let it pass by." "No", they all told me, and laughed, "You cannot stop the train." When the train came, I stood at the edge of the platform, facing the direction from which it came. I held up both my hands and said: "Stop!" The engine driver smiled as he passed me and then — the train stopped. The doors opened. We all got out of the rain and into the train. At St. Ives the engine driver called down from his cab as I passed him: "Goodbye now, and have a nice afternoon!"

———

Another vacation experience was Helmel in Bavaria. Helmel was a very original place; it was well organised and we had a very tight schedule all through the day, or most of it. At 7.00 in the morning the guests, about a dozen of us, had to go down to the exercise room to play medicine ball and do gym. The very first day when I took the medicine ball in my hand, I couldn't even hold it for one minute — it seemed so heavy. Later I learned to manage it, and I was not only very surprised but very thrilled when, after a week, I was able to do the required exercises with it: lift it up over my head, let it roll down my neck and back, and then catch it. Or hold it behind me with both hands and then throw it over my body to my partner who had to catch it. We did all kinds of exercises with this ball, and I not only got acquainted with it but also enthusiastic.

After an hour of this we had breakfast, and after that, which was about 9.00 or 9.30, we were sent back to bed. That, I thought, was the best moment of the day. Then the owner of the place brought a hot hay sack, put it on us, wrapped us up in woollen blankets, closed the curtains and told us to go back to sleep until she came to wake us up again. At about 11.00 she woke us up, told us to come down to the exercise room for some more exercises, different this time: singing in a choir and talking exercises which was supposed to be for better breathing. After that came lunch, and in the afternoon one was free. We took beautiful walks through the pine forests. We were there over Christmas and there was deep snow, over our knees, which we walked through. Christmas right in the country was a beautiful sight with decorated trees in front of the peasant houses.

Another vacation was in the Harz mountains. We took beautiful walks through the forests, and here also we met the Pendulum Lady, something new and fascinating for us. It is difficult to describe her, but I got one of those pendulums and started to use it over my dinner plate whenever

I wanted to find out whether I should eat the food or not. It almost became an addiction. When we went to another hotel and I started using it at our table, the people from the next table got interested, came over, and asked me to try it over their cider — it was very tempting to use it over everything. Interestingly enough, it seemed to make sense. If it said to me 'Don't eat this, it isn't good for you' it was usually right. Those were the foods I wasn't supposed to eat, and really knew I shouldn't.

———

Glenthorne in Grasmere was another favourite of ours. Cläre had already been there many times before I met her, and she was now very happy to show me that Quaker guest-house in the Lake District. The first time we went there together was in 1971. We went by train as far as Windermere and from there took a bus to Grasmere. Cläre was so happy and joyful and anxious to show me Glenthorne that she made us leave the bus at the wrong stop. We got out with our suitcases, and as soon as the bus had gone, Cläre looked around and said "Oh my! We got off too early. What shall we do now? How can we get to Glenthorne? There is no store or restaurant around here from where we could call for help. No public telephone anywhere."

Here we stood, on the road, and there were only small houses like one finds on the outskirts of a village. As Cläre thought it would be about a half hour's walk, we surely couldn't carry our suitcases there, so I suggested that we should just cross the street, ring the bell at one of those small houses, and ask the people if we could leave our cases there, and that's what we did. Then we started to walk; it was 7.00 o'clock when we arrived, tired and wet.

We told the manager what we had done, and he asked for the name of the people with whom we had left the cases — but we didn't know. We hadn't asked them. We didn't even know the name of the street or the house number. After the evening meal, one of the guests offered to take us down in his car to try to locate our suitcases, and luckily we didn't have much trouble finding the house.

Glenthorne is unbelievably beautiful — a very good Quaker atmosphere and many possibilities of hiking — everything really perfect. But there too we had some adventures. One morning a friend of Cläre's picked us up in Glenthorne and took us to Kendal. After spending a nice day with this friend, he left us at a bus stop in one of the small towns

131

between Kendal and Grasmere, so that he wouldn't have to come all the way back to Glenthorne. It was a Sunday evening, and we waited directly by the bus stop, which was in a public park. There we sat on the bench and waited for the bus ... and waited ... and waited. By now it was 10.00 o'clock, and we started to study the timetable, only to discover that on Sunday there was no bus. So what now? It was already dark and there we were in a strange town. We went to the main street, but being Sunday, no store was open. I suggested to try to hitch-hike in a private car, but Cläre didn't want that, so we went to the Police Station and rang the bell. No answer.

Then we found a man lying under his car in front of his house, apparently repairing it. We asked him if there was any taxi stand anywhere, and he said, "No, but there is a taxi man in the town", and he took us to the man's house. We rang the bell, but no answer. Now this young man, who had taken us to the taxi man's house, felt sorry for us. By now it was already after 11.00, and he said: "Well, I guess I'll have to take you to the next town where you can still reach a bus. But you'll have to wait a minute. I have my wife at home with a new baby. I cannot leave her at home all alone with the new baby. I have to take her and the baby along." He went into the house and got his wife and the baby, and we all got into his car. We drove for about half an hour to the next town, where he thought we could catch a bus to Grasmere.

We arrived at the town, and he got out of the car to be sure that we could catch a bus there. Then he came back to the car with the news that the bus had left three minutes ago. We had just missed it. "But the bus will stop on the way, and I can drive fast, so I think we will be able to catch it somewhere", he said. So off we went, trying to catch the bus, and after a while he thought he could see the bus far ahead. "We might catch it - we might catch it", he said. Time went by and we were chasing that bus, but after a while he said "Since I've taken you this far, I might as well take you right up to Grasmere, so you won't have to walk from Grasmere up to Glenthorne; that's a pretty long walk in the dark."

So this man, with the new baby and the young wife, drove us all the way up to Glenthorne. We arrived at 12.30 at night, and when Cläre tried to give him some money to pay for his petrol at least, he refused to take it. We had quite a time to get the wife to accept some money to buy something for her new baby. Of course we knew that one shouldn't judge people by their outward appearance, one shouldn't judge young people by their untidy sweaters, their long beards, and their unkempt long hair.

Here we had the proof of it again - a young man, who, by outward appearance looked pretty neglected, but who had a heart of gold.

———

For several years in succession, Cläre and I went to Garschorn, a beautiful place in the Austrian mountains. It is at 3,000ft altitude, and from there we could go on beautiful hikes. We could also take bus rides higher up the mountain. One summer we went to Lenk in Switzerland in the Berner Oberland. Lenk is also 3,000ft up, and as it was Cläre's wish, we took a ski-lift higher up still. It was the first time in her life that she rode in one of these, but she was so enthusiastic that we had to do it again the next day. Up there, at an altitude of 6,000 ft, we took a long hike with a beautiful view of the mountain ranges — quite an adventure for a woman of her age (91).

20/10/93

ILKA

CHAPTER 10

THE LAST CHAPTER

My brother's funeral

IT HAPPENED TO BE A FRIDAY; and it happened to be the 13th. I am not superstitious but what a gloomy day this was: the day of my brother's funeral. In the morning we were at the crematorium, in the afternoon at a memorial service. We, the closest family, intended to have the evening meal in my flat, but when I came home at 5.00 pm, anxious to prepare a meal for us all, I could not get in to my kitchen. The kitchen door was jammed. I called the caretaker, but he could not open the door. I called up my sister in her hotel. I told her that we, my friend and I, would join her, my other brother and my nephew, in their hotel for a meal. When, at about 9.00 pm, we were ready to go back home, my brother said: "Wait right here in the restaurant. We will go upstairs and get your coats for you." No sooner had they left than the fire alarm went off. Everybody scrambled out of the dining room, and rushed towards the doors. "Come, Cläre", I said, "We must walk down the back stairs to the ground floor."

Cläre was 92, I was 82. I had had an accident not long before and was walking with a stick. It seemed a long and difficult descent; young people, dashing down, overtook us and almost knocked us down, but we managed to get out of the hotel. Then we stood there in the street for thirty minutes. It was bitterly cold and wet, a mixture of snow and rain. We were without coats, scarves or gloves, and I was very worried in case my sister and brother were searching for us in the hotel. In fact, while we were standing outside in the cold, my brother was in the hall with our coats over his arm.

Cläre's last years

Two years later, in the autumn of 1984, Cläre and I decided to go once more to Rimberg for a week or two. We had been there in May and were happy to be back, but on the very first night, Cläre had a stroke. The doctor wanted to send her to a hospital. I told the doctor right away that I would let Cläre go to the hospital only if I could be admitted also, as her companion, and be in the same room with her. This was agreed, and Cläre was very well cared for, thankful and happy that I could be with her.

After five weeks Cläre was discharged from the hospital and we went back to her house in Lindorf, but her walking was poor and we got a physiotherapist to come in twice a week. We managed fairly well, but then on Christmas Eve, as Cläre was standing at the window to look at the beautifully decorated Christmas tree of the neighbours, she had another fall. I wanted to call the doctor of course, but Cläre wouldn't let me. She insisted that one shouldn't call a doctor out in the Christmas week - the doctor should have an undisturbed week. So we waited. Finally on the 2nd January 1985 I insisted on calling the doctor. He came, examined Cläre and said she would have to go to hospital. After about ten days there, Cläre herself said that she didn't want to go back to her own house any more.

As there was a new nursing home opening, attached to the hospital, Cläre was transferred to a private room there. Now I travelled back and forth between York and Düsseldorf. I always stayed three weeks in Lindorf so I could visit Cläre all day and every day, and then I would go back to England for a week or two to look after my flat in York.

When May came, Cläre said: "How about our summer vacation? Aren't we going to have a summer vacation this year?" "Oh", I said, "You want a summer vacation?" "Yes", said Cläre, "Of course I want a summer vacation. Can't we go?" So I promised Cläre to take her on a summer vacation and suggested that we go to Sonnmat - a very nice Sanatorium above Lucerne in Switzerland. I told the Head Sister in the nursing home that I was going to take Cläre on vacation in June. "What!" the Head Sister said, "You cannot do that! You have no right to say that. You cannot just decide that Mrs Stölting is going on vacation. The doctor has to decide that. The doctor has to give permission. You cannot do that." But I told her that I <u>was</u> going to take Cläre - that Cläre was going to have a vacation in June. Some days later I was told: "The doctor wants to see Mrs Stölting." I took Cläre with a wheelchair to the doctor's office. There we sat in the waiting room and waited our turn. Then the doctor came in. "Mrs Stölting, please." I said: "May I come in with her?" "No", said the doctor in a gruff voice, "You may not." He took the wheelchair into his surgery, and five minutes later he came out without Cläre. "Mrs Stölting is not going on vacation", he said. "Why not?" I said. "First of all", he said, "it's much too dangerous." "What is dangerous about it?" I said. "Her advanced age." I said: "Doctor, I don't think it makes any difference where Mrs Stölting dies. It is her wish to go on vacation, and I am taking her." "No", he said, "She cannot go". "Doctor", I said, "I am sorry, but I am taking Mrs Stölting. If you want me to I can give it to you in writing that I am taking her against your wishes." So that is what happened. He made me sign a note that I was taking her out against the wishes and orders of the doctor.

I had found out that we could travel from Düsseldorf to Lucerne without changing trains, but it was a long trip: ten hours. I suggested that we should travel first class. "Why first class?" said Cläre, "We don't belong in the first class." I said: "Cläre, it is a long trip, and in first class there are fewer passengers, you have more space, you will be able to stretch out on the seats and take a little nap, and the seats are more comfortable." "No" said Cläre, "No, I am not going to travel first class." "Why not?" I asked. "There aren't any nice people in first class with whom you can have a conversation. I have never travelled first class, and I am not going to start now." So we travelled second class.

After ten hours on the train, we finally arrived at Lucerne at 7.00 pm. For the last two hours, a friendly middle-aged Swiss couple had been in the same compartment with us. They had offered to help us get our baggage off the train at Lucerne. The friendly farmer had unloaded all our luggage, and now he stood on the platform to help Cläre off the train. There she stood looking down on to those three narrow and very steep steps, and was scared, both her hands clenched tightly to the iron railings. The kind farmer was holding out his arms towards her. "I will help you down," he said. But Cläre would not let go. I stood behind her, trying to persuade her, but no! She would not step down. We all three of us stood there as if nailed to the floor. Then I said: "Cläre, put your arms around the man's neck. Embrace him." That did it! Cläre embraced the farmer and he lifted her down from the train with a happy smile. Cläre was 93. It was her last and very happy vacation.

When we returned to the nursing home after four weeks, the doctor said: "It was a good idea that Mrs. Stölting went on vacation." He had a good reason for saying that: she was in much better health when she returned than she had been before she left. But soon it became Cläre's urgent wish that she and I should live together under the same roof, so I had to think about how we could arrange that. Cläre wasn't well enough any more to come to live with me in my flat in Tuke House, York, but we had to find a solution. Then I heard about the Rosenhof, a residential home for elderly people.

The Rosenhof also had a nursing department with 35 beds, but they wouldn't admit nursing cases directly from outside. I was able to talk the manager into agreeing to the following proposal: Cläre would have a room in the nursing department, where she would be just for the nights, while during the daytime she would be in my small flat one floor higher, and I would take care of her. The flat had a living-room, a bathroom and a kitchenette, and we furnished it with some things from her own house. It served as our living area during the day, and I slept on the couch in our living room at night. It really worked quite well: in the morning at 8.30 I went downstairs and took Cläre in her wheelchair up to the flat, and she spent all day with me in our living room. She had her main meal with me in the restaurant, and also the evening meal for the first few months, until she wasn't well enough to stay up that long.

Rosenhof had quite a nice garden where I always took her in her wheelchair. In the morning I got up at 6.30, went down to the very nice swimming pool in the basement, then had my own breakfast in my little kitchenette, and at 8.30 I called for Cläre. Every morning, when I entered the nursing wing's dining room and she saw me, she said: "It's good you are here." She was so happy and grateful for my being there; it was a really good arrangement.

We came to the Rosenhof in September 1985. Seven months later, on the 21st April 1986, Cläre died. In Cläre I lost a very good friend, but the friendship has outlasted her death. I still feel her presence very strongly. Very often I think: 'What would Cläre have done now?' Yes, it always still is as if Cläre is here; she actually lives with me in spirit, though she is gone in body. Sometimes we did have our little squabbles. I remember on one such occasion, when I said: "Cläre, tomorrow you'll be sorry", and she said: "I'm sorry already." Once I asked Cläre "What is the most important thing in a friendship?" and she said: "Warmth", adding: "One should always be aware of what the other person does not like, so that one doesn't do it", but a minute later she said: "No, that isn't right, that isn't enough. One should always be aware of what makes the other person happy, so that one always does things that do make the other person happy."

———

138

'Grief' 1986

In June 1986 I returned to my own flat in York, but very soon another heart-rending period in my life started. Eileen Booth, a very good friend to me and and many other people, fell ill with cancer. She spent her last 22 weeks in York District Hospital, and was a shining example of inner discipline and good morale to the nursing staff, to her visitors, to everybody. She will always live on in the hearts of those who knew her.

It was also in the year 1986 that I took up painting again, and writing stories which were printed in short volumes under the title 'Loose Leaves'. They became the basis of this autobiography, which I started with the encouragement of a friend, who had also edited the last four volumes of 'Loose Leaves'. Then, in December 1990, I moved into Lamel Beeches, a newly-opened residence for elderly frail people. Being nearly 89 I qualified for the 'elderly' part, though I did not feel frail. In making this move I was thinking that there might come a time when I would need help of some kind — and it came.

A sight problem

One morning in March 1993 I woke up and found I couldn't see the clock on the wall any more. In fact, I couldn't see anything clearly any more. Everything was as if in a thick fog. I went to see a consultant, who told me that my eyesight had deteriorated very quickly and severely. I would have to accept being like this always. That was a very big shock at first, but soon I told myself: 'I will not sit in a rocking chair and do nothing. I will stay as independent and active as possible.' I really adjusted quite well to the new situation, although there were days when I felt very bad about it, as this page from my diary shows:

> I am tired. I am weary. I am not in good spirits. How could I be? I feel fed up with this condition of poor vision. I want to see smiling faces, but I see no faces at all unless the person stands very close to me. Then they usually stare, as if to say 'Here I am'. Of course it is no good complaining. I have to learn to adapt myself to the outside world. I am receiving help in many little ways, for which I am grateful.

My loss of sight happened so suddenly, and came as such a big shock, that there was little time for grieving. After six weeks the grieving was over and I had to find ways of coping. I took out my sketch book and pastels and said to myself: 'I'll find out what I can do.' Then I thought: 'I can paint by memory. I don't need eyes to see an apple.' So I drew the shape of an apple, then a pear, and next to it a banana. With the pastels I made the apple green on one side and yellow on the other, and then drew a dish underneath. To colour it all in I took my magnifying glass to see where the colours should go. The next sketch I did was of grapes, and then tulips. I knew what these looked like — I'd done a lot of abstracts before my eyes failed, so that was easy. I realised that I could paint anything.

Then I thought to myself: 'My whole body, my self, is a self-supporting community. I'm going to call an emergency meeting of the committee. My brain will be the chairman, and I'll give the chairman the floor.' The chairman greeted the members, and then said: "I have something important to tell you all. One of our members, the eyesight, has gone into semi-retirement. Its vision has done good and loyal work for over 90 years, and we all know that we are a democratic organisation. If one member is sick or goes on vacation, the other members have to share that one's work out between themselves. In our case, the hands are good at seeing and can take on a lot of the work by feeling. And if every member does a little more work than before, the whole organisation will run smoothly."

There are some things that I can actually do better now than before. For example, my room is in a corner of a dark corridor and I always had trouble locking and unlocking the door, since it was difficult to see. It always took me a long time to find the lock, and then I fidgetted trying to get the key in the right position in the lock. Now I don't try to see the lock; I know I can't see it. Now I use two fingers to hold the key in the right position, find the lock and insert the key. It's locked and unlocked in a jiffy.

The biggest shock was realising that I could no longer read at all. I can see things only through the corner of my eye; wherever I look there is nothing except a little bit at the side. When I went to a concert I found it very upsetting that the singer had no face. At my Quaker Meeting I couldn't see anybody, or the flowers on the table. I could see only shadows, although when it snowed it was beautiful because I could see more clearly thanks to all that extra light. I feel much happier out of doors, because when I come into a building it feels like a dark cellar. Some days I get fed up and think: 'I've had enough of this', but on the whole I've got used to seeing only shadows everywhere instead of people. Outside, where there is space, I don't feel so restricted. If someone approaches me I say: "Do I know you?" Of course one has some inhibitions about talking to people one doesn't recognise.

141

In town I only make my usual round; I know the places I want to go to, but in districts that I don't know, I'm not so happy. I've been to London twice by train since my eyesight got worse, and I waited at the barrier to be met, but I couldn't see the faces of any of the people, and I don't like standing around waiting in unfamiliar places like that.

My letter-writing is now better than it was at first: I write fluently on heavy black-lined paper and I'm even teaching myself to write on un-lined paper, though someone has to cross the t's and dot the i's for me. I would like to read my own mail, though; it's embarrassing to have it read to me. In fact, I suffer from a triple handicap: poor sight, poor hearing and old age. But there is also a funny side to these disabilities. One day the kind reader helping me with my mail stopped in the middle of a sentence, held the letter up in front of my face, and said: "Ilse, what's this word? I can't read it." Writing too has its lighter moments. I try to practise every day, and one day, after I had written a whole page, I found that the page was

It is good to be independent.
I tell my self: don't try it.
        just do it!

The light is right
The time is right!
The table - stable
The paper - ready
and my hand steady:
. Go!

7/12/93

142

empty. There was not a word on it. Why? Because I had used the wrong end of the pen. I had to laugh, and then said to myself: "Bravo! That was good! I've practised writing a whole page — without wasting any paper."

One day at the lunch table in our communal dining room, a neighbour expressed surprise that I hadn't noticed her absence at tea-time on the previous day. "You know that I can only see a very little", I said to her. "I can't see people who aren't there." Mostly I make myself a cup of tea in the pantry first thing in the morning, but it's not easy when you can't see clearly. An old friend gave me some advice: 'Hold the teapot over the cup and count ONE, TWO, THREE, STOP. I followed her advice and then reported progress: "One, two, three, stop. The cup is empty; not a drop." Maybe, I added, the pot was empty!

On the subject of handicaps (like poor vision) and how to deal with them, one of the most difficult things I've had to convey to the carers at Lamel Beeches is to refrain from telling me to 'be careful'. A handicapped person needs courage. If you tell them to be careful you make them insecure and then they become more hesitant, and have more accidents. If, when you learn to ride a bike, you feel insecure and are afraid of falling off, you start to wobble and you will fall off. If you have courage and go fast you are safe. Another thing I tell people is: if you're asked to do something which you think is difficult, don't ever say, or think, or feel: 'I will try to do it'. Just DO IT! Just by telling yourself 'I'll try' you make yourself insecure and hesitant, when what is needed is to act.

Some closing reflections

It was early in 1994 that my friends encouraged me to write my autobiography, though I was already over 90, and handicapped by poor vision. Everything has to be read to me, but otherwise I am leading a fairly normal life. I feel honoured and thankful to have good friends who so cheerfully and loyally help me, and the very fact that they support me and are enthusiastic about my writing and art work helps me to remain alive and active. However, when I began to write this autobiography, I faced several problems about what to put in and what to leave out. I have had a long life, with many ups and downs. Of course one has the inclination not to mention the dark episodes. I was brought up at a time when the reputation of a family was of the utmost importance, especially a so-called 'better' or upper-middle class family. As my parents' marriage was not a happy one, I was tempted to leave them out of my book. But parents and the home atmosphere have such a profound influence on one's whole development that it is impossible to leave them out.

Again, I found it very difficult to decide whether to write about some Jewish people and homes where I worked, and where I was not treated well. One doesn't like to say anything unflattering about a group of people to whom one belongs; where I found a Jewish family which was not a 'nice' family, it hurt me particularly, being Jewish myself. Of course I realise that religion doesn't make people 'good' or 'bad'. On the other hand, I think it's important not to hide these things either, to admit that Jews are like everyone else — a mixture of good and bad.

Another difficulty I experienced was whether to talk about the clinical depression suffered by some of my relations. People have asked me from time to time, even quite recently, what made me decide to live in York? I tend to say that it is because I like York; it's a very nice old town, a tourist city with many people from abroad, and one doesn't have the feeling of living in a small town. That is the truth — but it is not the whole truth.

144

What really brought me to York was a brother who was a patient in The Retreat, a Quaker hospital for the mentally ill. I had brought him there from New York in 1973. For the first six months I visited him every day, and as he was very attached to me, I decided to stay in York. Why is it, I wonder, that one shrinks from admitting mental illness in the family whereas the same would not be the case for any other kind of physical illness.

Where does the birth of a personality really start - with the actual birth of the person or long before? I feel that a personality is built up from particles of humanity coming together long before the person is born. Unfortunately, we know so little about our ancestors and their personalities. Of course one's personality changes all the time during one's life, because it is influenced by many things around one, by the circumstances in which one lives, even by the climate, the country, the people one meets. They too have a big influence, and so one can say that a personality is never really finished; like life itself, it always changes.

Another question relates to political beliefs and activities: should I avoid mentioning these in the book or should they be included, even at the cost of shocking some readers? Why does one want to write an autobiography? It could be for several different reasons. One reason might be to have something to leave behind for friends and relatives, for a future generation as a record of how life was at the beginning of the century. Another reason could be educational or therapeutic. When did my life begin, I wonder, and when does it end? I am sure it began before the date of my birth, and will not end with the date of my death. I feel I am just a small, small part in the whole big chain of humanity, which is always flowing and never ending.

145

CHAPTER 11

IN SICKNESS AND IN HEALTH

LOOKING BACK ON MY LIFE, I find it is really true that there is usually something good in everything bad that happens, only at the time one doesn't realise it. In my own case, I would never have found World Fellowship if I hadn't been sick and needed a place for convalescence. I was working in St. Barnabas House at the time, and asked the housekeeper if she knew anywhere I could go. She had just received some literature from World Fellowship, and said she would like me to go there and try it out for her. Again, I would never have known anything about Monhagan Island, that lovely little old fishing village and artists' colony, had it not been recommended by one of my fellow patients in the hospital.

Another example of good coming out of bad: I was discharged from hospital in Los Angeles after a bad accident, but wasn't well enough to take care of myself. My nephew saw Meadowlark advertised in one of the papers, called them to make a reservation for me, and drove me there, a two-hour journey. When we got there and I walked into the office, supported by a cane and limping, the receptionist said: "Oh, I'm sorry, we cannot take you." I said: "Oh, but we have made a reservation." She said: "Yes, but we were told you needed a place after a stay in hospital; we didn't expect you still to be in such a condition. I don't think you are well enough to participate in our programme. Your room is in one of the cottages some way away from the main house, and the path is very uneven. The handicrafts are done in a different cottage again, very difficult to get to. And the dining room is in the basement with very steep stairs down. I don't think you are well enough."

While I was arguing with the receptionist, another lady came into the office. She was the assistant of Dr Loomis, the owner and manager of Meadowlark. "What is the problem here?" she asked. The receptionist

147

told her, and she said to me: "May I try you out?" I said: "Yes of course, please do." "All right", she said, "First we will see if you can make the path to your cottage." We went to the cottage, then we came back to the main house, and when I was confronted by the steep stairs going down to the dining room, I just turned round and walked down backwards. That I could do. Then we walked down to the workshops. Finally the director's assistant said: "I don't see any problem. I think you'll be all right." And so I was accepted into Meadowlark.

———

Most people have health problems at some time during their lives, and I have had my share. In the year 1936 I had been nursing a patient with pneumomia day and night for ten days. When the patient was out of danger, I decided to take some days off because I had been feeling poorly myself for some days. I thought that it was just the result of over-work and over-stress. I called up a friend of mine, who suggested taking me to a furnished room right in the centre of New York so that she could send me her own general practitioner (at that time I lived in the suburbs). I accepted her offer, and climbed the four flights of stairs to the new room. The same afternoon the doctor came, and after examining me, he said: "You have pleurisy; besides that you have an acute gall bladder infection; besides that you are having a nervous breakdown — but otherwise you are all right. I will write a prescription for you." I asked the doctor to do me a favour and drop it off at the pharmacy. And so I took care of myself for the next three days.

Each day I had to wash myself and change my pyjamas, which had been soaked by perspiration and high fever every night. Three times a day I stood in front of my big mirror trying to get the prescribed mustard plasters on the right places on my back. On the third day, just while I was standing naked in front of the mirror, the door opened and in walked the doctor. I said: "I am sorry, doctor, I didn't expect you to come just now." The doctor said: "Apparently it is a good thing when the doctor comes in unexpectedly. Tell me, who is taking care of you?" I said: "Doctor, I am a trained nurse. I am taking care of myself." He said: "No, Miss Karger, you cannot be the nurse and the patient at the same time. And besides, who is taking care of your nourishment? Who is feeding you?" I said: "The nourishment is no problem; I am not hungry. I am just drinking water." "No", the doctor said, "I will send an ambulance and take you to the hospital." "Doctor", I said, "This is not an emergency. If you think that I should go to the hospital, I will go tomorrow morning by taxi, but not now by ambulance."

The next morning I felt very, very sick, and I didn't feel like travelling in the taxi all by myself, so I called up another friend on the phone. When she heard my voice she said: "Ilse! Are you still alive?" "Yes", I said, "But I am ready to go to the hospital, and I was going to ask if you could escort me, because I don't feel like going by myself." "Yes", she said, "I will come." On the way to the hospital in the taxi I fainted, and when I opened my eyes again, I found myself lying on a bed in the hospital with my winter coat on, and around my bed were standing a lot of people, including my friend, who looked very pale. I said to her: "Why do you look so pale? You look awful." "Yes, Ilse", she said, "you gave us all a terrible shock." I was a patient in that hospital for almost four weeks, and when they discharged me, the doctor said to me: "You know, if you had come just three or four minutes later, we would not have been able to bring you back to life."

———

On another occasion I was in hospital in New York, on the operating table. A pretty Indian woman wearing a sari under her white doctor's coat was ready to give me the anaesthetic. She introduced herself, then said: "Will you please count for me?" "No", I said, "Why count?" "Please do count" she said. "No, I will not count. I will tell you a story instead." And I embarked on my story, a true story from life, my life with children. I don't know how far I got with my story, but the next day the nice Indian doctor came into my ward. I was surprised to see her. "Well", she said, "You told me a lovely story yesterday. Now I have come to hear the end of it."

———

It was while I was living in New York, and between jobs, that I turned Maria, an unemployed fashion designer, into a nurse overnight, so to say. Maria had come from Vienna in the hope of getting settled in New York. She was young and pretty, and every day she went out to look for work, but could not find any. Then one day my Nurses Registry called me up. They knew that I specialised in nursing infants and children but they wanted me to do them a favour. The patient to be nursed was an elderly woman who had been in the hospital with pneumonia, and now needed help at home. I agreed to go if they could not find anyone else within the next two hours, but then an idea hit me: Maria could do it. I went to see her.

"Maria", I said, "Here is good news: a job for you." "But I am not a nurse", she said. I explained that in the USA anybody who puts on a white uniform could call herself a 'practical nurse', and I assured her that she could do it. Then I called up my Registry again. "I have found a nurse for that elderly lady, but she is not a trained nurse. Shall I send her to your office?" "Oh no, Miss Karger, that is not necessary if you recommend her." Now I went to work on Maria. I taught her how to read a thermometer and how to take a pulse; I told her that all she would really have to do is to be friendly, be nice and pleasant, to cheer up the patient, give her nice meals and make her comfortable. "Tonight when you come home", I added, "Call in and report. If for any reason you feel that you cannot do it, then I will go there tomorrow as your substitute." I gave Maria one of my white uniforms, a thermometer, and my watch, and sent her off with my good wishes. Late in the evening she was at my door. "Ilse, she wanted mustard. I tried to talk her out of it, but she said that they always gave it to her in the hospital." Of course, the patient had meant mustard plaster. I briefed Maria on the use of that, after which she and her patient got on very well. Maria took care of her patient for three weeks at $20 per week, and was very happy to do so.

———

My Nurse's Registry had called me up. "Are you free? We have a case for you. It's only for one week to relieve the permanent nurse who is sick with flu." They gave me the address, a big Victorian house, old and dilapidated. I rang the bell. An old woman opened the door. "Are you the nurse? I am Bella, the housekeeper. I have been with Mrs Young since her daughter was born. I was her nurse, and she is 55 now. I will take you upstairs." Old Bella held on to the banisters and actually had to pull herself up. There she handed me over to Anne, Mrs Young's daughter, who said: "I will take you to the nurse's room. She has been here for three years; she will tell you all you need to know." Anne took me as far as the nurse's door, knocked on the door, then went away. "Come in", called the nurse. As I entered her room, she said: "Close the door quickly. I have to talk to you." I liked the nurse's room; it was a large, sunny room, with a nice big bed. But why was it so stuffy and overheated? And why was the nurse lying in bed with a heavy wool cardigan on top of a wool pullover? And those two woollen scarves, one wound around her neck, the other one around her head? Her face was flushed.

"I am not sick", said the nurse, "I am playing sick. The ambulance will come and take me to the hospital. That is the only way for me to get out of here. I cannot take it any more — the dirt, I can't stand it! But the people here are so nice — I just could not tell them that I wanted to leave, but I am telling you, so that you know you are now the permanent nurse. I am not coming back." Ten minutes later the ambulance arrived and the 'sick' nurse was carried out of the house on a stretcher while Old Bella and Anne stood at the door and wished her a quick recovery.

Mrs Young, the patient, was in her late eighties, and had been bed-ridden for five years, her whole right side paralysed. She could not do anything for herself and so this was a 24-hour nursing job. And what a job. Mrs Young was not in the least cooperative. The first morning, when I suggested giving her a sponge bath, she did not want to be washed, and she did not want to be undressed. I say 'undressed' because under her nightie she wore a big old-fashioned corset with fishbones and strings and also a white silk blouse with a high-neck collar and fishbones sewn into it. On her hair she always wore a lace cap which I was not allowed to remove, even to brush her hair. "My daughter takes care of that once a month", she said. And when her bed needed changing, she wanted me to put some newspaper under her so that she would not lie in the wet.

That first day she was really impossible. She just would not let me change the sheets. I stood at her bedside and said: "Please let me change your sheets." "No", she said, "It's my bed, and I don't want it changed." "I will just have to stand here and wait patiently until you let me do it", I said. "You can only talk to me like that because you are Jewish", my patient said, "Otherwise you would not dare to." In the evening it took two hours to get Mrs Young ready for the night, which she dreaded. She had 12 pillows in her bed, of different shapes and different sizes, and they had to be arranged in a special way. When I had, let's say, put pillow number four in her back, she would say: "Number two is not in the right spot. Start all over once more." And when I had arranged number nine she would say: "But number five does not feel right." Of course I realised that Mrs Young wanted to make the dreaded night as short as possible.

My day started at 6.00 am, but in the evening she would not let me start to get her ready for the night before 11.00 pm, and it took two hours. That meant that I was finished at 1.00 am, and I also had to attend to her once or twice during the night. Being always 'on call' meant I had to sleep in her room, on a couch, so I didn't see much of that nice, bright room called the nurse's room. As I did not get enough sleep, I started to use a trick. In the afternoon I would move her clock forward two hours, so we made preparations for the night from 9.00 pm to 11.00 pm. Of course I always turned the clock back afterwards, as I would not have wanted to start the day at 4.00 am; 6.00 am seemed early enough!

After eight days a letter from the 'sick' nurse came to say that her doctor did not want her to work any more. Mrs Young asked me to stay on, but I could refuse with a clear conscience, as I had promised to act as maternity nurse for a young woman. I stayed one whole month with Mrs Young, though; she had now got used to me and seemed to like me. When I left, she asked me to get her another nurse, but only a Jewish nurse, she said.

———

It was my first day in the hospital. I was awaiting a major operation, the last bed in a room with four beds. In the evening the Ward Sister came in, stood in front of the first patient, put her hand in her pocket, took out a pill, said: "Open your mouth", and threw it into the patient's mouth. This performance was repeated for the next two patients, but when she came to my bed, I told her I wouldn't take a pill, as the doctor hadn't seen me yet, and hadn't prescribed anything. The next evening, when the Sister came into the room, I was prepared. She went to bed number one: "Open your mouth." In flew the pill, and so on at the next bed, and the third. Then she came to my bed. As she put her hand into her pocket, I said to her: "Open your mouth!" and into her mouth I threw a candy wrapped in paper. The Sister stumbled back, then caught herself, and said: "That wasn't a very nice thing to do." "No", I said, "It wasn't, but that is what you do every night." The next night, and every night after that, the pills were handed to the patients out of small plastic cups, and strangely enough, my relationship with that Sister became a very friendly one.

Two days after my operation, the night nurse shook me by the shoulder: "Wake up, wake up!" "But why?" "We need your help. There is an old man just coming out of the anaesthesia, and we can't manage him. Please come. Do you talk Yiddish?" "No, I don't. What made you think that I could talk Yiddish?" "Because you talk French." I had been an interpreter for three patients, a young French girl in my own ward, a French lady in the next room, and an Italian man further down the corridor. Now Mr Keller was in the hospital for the first time in his life. He did not talk English. He was an Orthodox German Jew, and he was very upset because the nurses could not understand him. In their desperation they had got me to help them.

Well, it was not an easy task. I stood in front of Mr Keller, who wanted to get of the bed, while those two nurses tried to hold him in bed. "Mr Keller", I said, "Tell me, what is the trouble?" "I want to go to the toilet, and they will not let me go. I am a decent person; I will <u>not</u> wet my bed. They can put that rubber thing back in when I come back from the toilet." I tried to explain the function of the catheter, but Mr Keller did not understand. He kept on saying: "I will not wet the bed; just let me go." I went to the foot of his bed, took the chart which was hanging there, and said: "Mr Keller, listen to me please. Here is what the doctor wrote down. I will read you what it says. It is the doctor's orders." And I read: "Mr Keller must wet his bed tonight. He is not allowed go to the toilet." The problem was solved.

The night before the French lady in the single room next door was due to have her major operation, I thought it would be nice to give her a 'farewell dinner'. I arranged the chairs in our ward in a semi-circle, with hers at the place of honour, and we invited her to bring her meal in so we could all eat together. Right in the middle of our 'celebration' the door opened, and in came the hospital's Chief Medical Officer. This was a woman; in fact, all the medical staff here were women, the only hospital in New York like that. "What's going on here?" she asked. I explained about our neighbour, and the farewell dinner. "Good for you!" said the Chief Medical Officer, and went out again. The next morning we formed a guard of honour for her outside the lift that was to take her to the operating theatre, and though she was already drowsy from the anaesthetic, she told us later that she had felt really supported.

When I was discharged after four weeks, the Ward Sister said: "The hospital shouldn't let you go; you are good for the patients' morale, and that helps us so much."

———

Since coming to live in York some 25 years ago, I have been taken to the Accident & Emergency Department of the District Hospital five times . Every time the doctors wanted to keep me as an in-patient, and every time I had to fight not to be kept in. "I would be a very bad patient", I would say, "I don't take any pills or drugs, and I do not cooperate with any treatment." Then they would make me sign a paper, and I would leave the hospital 'against the doctor's advice'.

On the first occasion, I had had a heart attack in a restaurant. The restaurant called for an ambulance without my consent, but the driver refused to take me to my flat. He said: "The hospital sent us out to get you, and we are not allowed to return without you!"

The second time, I fell in the street and cracked some ribs, but the worst accident I had was my own fault. I had been shopping, and was in a great hurry to get home and give my cleaning lady a piece of her favourite pastry and cream for her coffee break. I crossed the main street, but not at a traffic light, and sure enough, I was knocked down by a car. My head bounced on the road like a rubber ball; I felt it hit the ground three times. Then I was picked up with a splitting headache, but still worried about the cake; it would be spoilt by being taken to the hospital.

I gave somebody my telephone number. "My cleaning lady will answer the phone", I said. "Tell her that I am delayed, and will be home a little later." In the ambulance, the attendant told me that I had a cracked skull, but that was not the case. I only had a bad case of concussion, and a large lump the size of a grapefruit on the back of my head. I refused to stay in the hospital as a patient, and they would not send me home by ambulance, so I had to go by taxi. After that, my nature practitioner attended to me.

I have now been under the care of a nature practitioner for 18 years and I must honestly say that my general health is much better now than it was 20 years ago. I think the basic difference between a medical doctor and a nature practitioner is that the doctor treats the symptoms which are the result of the sickness, the symptoms which show up, which you complain about, while the nature practitioner will look for the cause of the sickness. The symptoms might help in that they give him guidance of where to look for the cause, but he will always be interested in finding the cause of your trouble, and to remedy that; he will not use pain-killers at all. Also I have found that a nature practitioner is not so much interested in patching up sick people as he is in keeping them healthy.

———

In the 1970s in York, at 8.00 o'clock on a cold winter morning, I was in bed and thought I heard the telephone. Out of bed I jumped and ran down the long corridor into the living room to pick up the phone. With no chair in reach, I decided to sit on the floor, but not realising that a different movement was needed, I fell on the floor with a terrific bump. I really was hurt. I couldn't even get up by myself, but I still had the phone in my hand, so I called up a neighbour, and asked her to come and help me. The hospital sent an ambulance, and I was given an X-ray, which showed that nothing was broken, but I had a terrible pain in my hip. The hospital sent me back home with a note to the local doctor and a bottle of pain killers, telling me to call the doctor on Monday and ask for a house visit.

154

On Monday the doctor came round and asked me to show him the bottle of pain-killers. "This is not enough", he said, "You need many more pain-killers. I will write out a prescription." He didn't even look at my hip, but said: "Stay in bed until I come for another visit". When I asked him when that would be, he said: "In ten days." The next day I called up my nature practitioner, who had been away for the week-end. He came the same day, in his lunch time, knelt down in front of the settee, and looked at my hip. Then he took my leg and swung it around. I said: "You are hurting me terribly." "Yes", he said, "I know, but I have to do it." Another swinging around with my leg and a big jerk, and then he said: "I think it will be all right now." "What do you think was wrong?" I asked. "It was dislocated, but now it is back in." He was right; after two days all was well again.

———

Nowadays the dangers of smoking are common knowledge, but not so when I lit my first cigarette, in Vienna as a student nurse. The professor of that nursing school told his students: "When you go on night duty you will find that in the middle of the night comes a time when you can scarcely keep your eyes open and your mind on the job. Then take five minutes off, go out into the fresh air, and smoke a cigarette. That will revive you." I followed the professor's advice. I started to smoke. Soon I would smoke a cigarette after every meal, and one the minute I went off duty. This went on for 32 years. Then all of a sudden my brain, which was smarter than I was, said: "Stop! I will not take any more of it." I went to see my doctor, but the doctor was not on my side. "You'll have to stop", he said. And that was it; I never lit another cigarette.

———

As I woke up early in the morning from a healthy deep sleep some while ago, the thought came to me that the human body is a wonderful piece of art, a heavenly creation. The whole body functions as one big whole unit; all parts of it pull together, hand in hand, around the clock. While I sleep at night and rest my bones, my muscles and my mind, my inner organs keep on working for me in their quiet steady rhythm without my being aware of it. My heart, my lungs, my kidneys, my glands and so on, they are all on the job in quiet unity. They might even do a little mending here and there, some repair work while I sleep peacefully. What a wonderful instrument the human body is. We should be really grateful. We should appreciate it. We should not take it for granted. We should care for it and not abuse it. We should listen to its wishes and respect its needs. It has its natural life-cycle. Why is it that we are careful with inanimate objects, which we have bought for a lot of money, and value them, while the most precious gift that was given to us, our own self, we do not treat with respect?

CHAPTER 12

ENCOUNTERS AND RELATIONSHIPS

Encounters

IN 1933, WHEN I WAS ON MY WAY from Berlin to Switzerland, I decided to stop over at Heidelberg. I arrived late in the evening, and checked in to a hotel. The next morning I got up at 5.00 o'clock to have a look at that old historic university town, but found dear old Heidelberg still asleep. No one was in the streets; the stores were all closed; the wooden shutters shut tightly. I wanted to get to the market place as that is usually the heart of these old towns, but I had no idea in which direction to walk. I had no city map. I was overjoyed to see an old peasant-woman standing at a street corner. 'She will tell me', I thought, and what a friendly smile she had when I approached her. "Yes", she said, "I'll show you. Come with me." Together we crossed the road, and there to my surprise stood a big basket, a handle on each side. "You take one side", she said, "And I'll take the other." Together we carried her asparagus to the market!

———

I had been sent to nurse the two little girls of a young couple who had arrived only six months earlier from their native Italy. The children had come down with a bad case of measles, and whooping cough on top of that. I was kept very busy, day and night, for two weeks. Their cook, Alice, came from South Africa. She belonged to a religious sect called 'Father Divine', whose centre was in New York, and whose official greeting, used by all the members, was: "Peace!". She had been sent by her church, and tried to please her employers, and to get used to American-Italian compromises in cooking. She always smiled.

157

The couple were polite when Alice served that African-style salad which they found hard to chew; I found it trying when I came down to the kitchen in the morning, tense because I had had to leave the children alone while getting their breakfasts, and found Alice sitting in her rocking chair, rocking back and forth while reading her sect's newspaper. With a gentle smile she would look up and say: "Peace". Whenever I came down to the kitchen to get something I was greeted by "Peace". Alice was always sitting in her rocking chair, and I had to wait for her to get the children's meals ready. I was not allowed to do that myself; it would have been regarded as trespassing on her domain.

I could see that Mr and Mrs Tomas were not happy with Alice. "Alice is a nice person", Mrs Tomas said, "But her cooking is really hard to digest. Still, as she is so polite and willing, I don't have the heart to give her notice." I went to have a word with Alice: "Are you happy here?" I asked her, and Alice replied: "Father Divine takes care of me. He sent me here, and it's my duty to obey him. I don't have the right to leave until I am told to." Some days after this, Alice came to me jubilantly. "I am so happy! I am so happy! My prayers have been answered!" "What happened?" I asked. "I can leave this job! I can go home to Father Divine. Mrs Tomas told me to go", she said. I had been able to play 'providence' for both sides.

———

I was on my way back from Florida to New York. It was an overnight trip on the train. There was only one person besides me in my compartment, a young woman. She was crying. "What happened to you?" I asked her. "I lost my suitcase with everything in it." "It will be found, I am sure", I said, and went to the train conductor. He called up the station where she had checked the suitcase in, and there it was found.

It was a long journey. We arrived in New York at 7.00 am the next morning, a Sunday. It was bitterly cold. Though already the 1st of April, it was snowing heavily. "Let's go into a cafeteria and have breakfast", I suggested. I knew that she had to face another night on the train to get home to Canada, and that she did not know anybody in New York. "What will you do today? You need a rest", I said. "I will go to a movie, I think; there I can sleep, as it's dark while the show is on", she said. "You had better come home with me", I said. I took her home with me. 'Home' was a furnished room in the flat of an old lady. As soon as we arrived I made my guest comfortable. I let her have a warm bath, and then put her in my bed, thinking that she needed the rest more urgently than I did.

158

I had been on the train all night, that's true, but she had already been travelling for two nights, and had to be on a train for a third night.

Then I called up my sister and told her I was back in New York. "Since when?" asked my sister. "Since ten minutes", I said. "Come over for lunch", said my sister. "I can't." "Why not?" "I have a visitor." "How can you have a visitor if you just came home? Who is your visitor?" "I met her on the train." "And where is she now?" "In my room." "Then you'd better go back to your room in a hurry, or tomorrow all your jewellery will be missing." Some 45 years later I asked a close friend of mine aged 93: "What do you consider to be the most important thing in life? What for are we in the world? What is the purpose of our life?" "To help as many people as possible", she replied.

———

I had spent my day off in New York and was on my way back to the small town out in the country where I was working in a school. It was midnight, and I was the only person to get off the train. I tried to call for a taxi from the public phone in front of the station, but got no answer. While I was still standing near the phone-booth, a police car pulled up. Two policemen bellowed at me: "What are you doing here all alone at this hour of the night?" Then they tried to get me a taxi, but there was no answer. I asked them: "Can you take me home to the Cottage School?" "No, we can only take you after something has happened to you. Nothing has happened to you yet." "Would you advise me to walk home through this forest by myself at this time?" "No." "What shall I do?" "We don't know." After that I gave them a talk. I told them that the police should protect unescorted women, and help them when they needed help, not wait until something had happened to them. They drove me home.

———

Many years later I had another late-night encounter. I had been visiting a friend in one of the suburbs of London, and had caught the last train back. When we got to Baker Street Station, which was not actually the station I wanted, all the lights went off in the train, and everybody had to get off. I followed the crowd to the street, but I was still a stranger in London, staying at the Friends International Centre. I had no idea in what direction to walk. I hailed a taxi. The taxi stopped, but when I told the driver where I wanted to go, he said: "That's not my direction." The same happened with the next taxi, and also with the third one. Then I

159

decided to stop a private car, but none would stop. They just whizzed by. 'I'd better walk to the next traffic light. Then I will have a chance', I thought. By now it was past midnight. I stood in the middle of the street. A big van stopped for the red light. I knocked on the window. "I am stranded", I said, "Can you help me?" "Go back to the kerb, I will pull up there." Doubtfully I went back on to the pavement, but the driver did pull up. He got down off his seat, came around, and helped me to climb up. But there was no seat beside the driver's seat. "Go inside the van, there you will find an old chair", he said, and then he took me right to the front door of the Friends International Centre, though it was out of his way. The next morning my room mates asked me: "How did you get home so late last night?" "I was delivered by the Daily Express", I said, and I really was: it was the Daily Express newspaper van that had brought me home.

———

There is a wholefood restaurant in York which opened an extension on the top floor. Cläre and I went there for lunch on the day they opened it. The manageress was busy behind the counter. Her young helper, was clearing the tables. I don't know why, but I ventured into the kitchen. It was a large beautiful kitchen, but what a mess! Cups, plates, forks and so on, all thrown into the sink together, which was full of dirty water. I went back to get my friend. "Cläre", I said, "Come with me. The kitchen needs us. There is work to be done." We washed the dishes; we swept the kitchen floor; we organised the kitchen. When the manageress appeared, she was surprised to see us. "I hope you don't mind that we invaded your kitchen", I said. "Not at all", she said with a friendly smile, "Everybody is allowed to come in and help." Well, we two self-appointed voluntary dishwashers went there for a whole week every day, and loved doing it. We were pretty sure we were the oldest dish-washers in York, Cläre at 90 and I at 80.

———

I once had an interesting experience in a health clinic where I was a patient. The dinner was served, and it looked very appetising, but as I approached the big potato with my knife, I found that it was very hard, and it was cold. As a matter of fact, it was a raw potato. 'That is strange', I thought, 'They've never given us raw potatoes before, but I have full confidence in this clinic, and they know what they are doing. If they give us a raw potato, it must have a reason.' I looked around at the other

160

patients. I noticed that everybody was looking around to find out what the others were doing — and then everybody ate their potato. The next day, I asked the doctor who was treating me: "Is there any special value in a raw potato?" And his answer was: "Yesterday there was a mistake in the kitchen. They forgot to put the potatoes into the oven." Well, I wonder; why did everybody eat that potato? Was it because they all had full confidence that the clinic knew what they were giving us, or was it that we human beings are like a herd of cattle, following the leader?

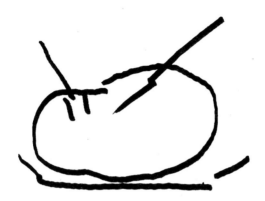

Relationships

Naturally, a good human relationship is a basic requirement in all dealings between people, but unfortunately this is sometimes overlooked. I was fully aware of the need to establish a good relationship in the private houses in which I worked, not only between me and my employers but more importantly in maternity work, between parents and the new child, and other children in the family. If you would ask me what are the most important credentials for living and working with children, I would say love and patience, seasoned with humour. The following stories will show what I mean.

Peter, one of the children in my nursery school, was a very nice boy, but rather quiet. I did not know that he had a little brother until one day his mother said to me: "Peter has a bad character. He does not like his baby brother." Later I questioned Peter. "Do you have a baby brother?" "Yes." "How old is he?" "Only six months." "What can he do?" "He

161

cannot even throw a ball straight." A week later the mother reported that the baby was sick in hospital, but Peter did not take any notice; he never asked about the baby. Two weeks later the mother came to see me again. "Here is the proof that Peter has a bad character", she said. "Yesterday when I told him that the baby is better, and coming home, he said: 'Mummy, couldn't we leave him in the hospital for good? Then I wouldn't always be late in the nursery school. You wouldn't have to give the baby his breakfast before taking me to school'". From Peter's point of view, the baby was just a big nuisance: he had to share his room with the baby, and when the baby was sleeping he was not allowed to go in. When it was awake, it got most of his mother's attention. Before the baby was born, Peter had been told by his mother: "You are lucky! You will soon have a brother to play with", but Peter could not see it that way.

In two cases where I was a maternity nurse I was told on arriving: "You must have nothing to do with the older child. Do not allow her to come into the nursery; she wants to throw the baby out of the crib." Needless to say, the big sisters became my helpers, and those infants their beloved babies. Then there was the family in New York with an adopted child. The Nurses Registry had sent me and said the mother was sick in the hospital with flu, and I would be needed for one week. On my arrival, the father opened the door. "My wife is in hospital with a nervous breakdown", he said, "Johnny is too much for her, though she loves him dearly." He handed me a bunch of typed pages. "This is Johnny's schedule", he told me. The schedule went something like this: 6.00 am toilet seat; 6.20 orange juice; 6.30 toilet seat; 7.00 am breakfast; 7.30 toilet, and so it went on. The father also told me that they had been on the waiting list for a long time, then suddenly one day they were informed by phone to come and get their baby. But they would have to get him the very next day, otherwise their name would be put on to the end of the waiting list again.

Johnny at 16 months seemed very lively, but he did not yet talk or walk. I had received some more instructions: 'Johnny must have the safety belt on in his pram because he stands up while one pushes the pram. His mittens must be pinned to his sleeves, so he cannot throw them down onto the ground. If you bring him into the living-room, everything that is breakable must be removed first.' Of course I ignored all those 'precautions', but I had to overcome some obstacles. The first obstacle was Granny, the father's mother. That first day Granny came in the afternoon and walked right into the nursery. She looked a funny figure, dressed all in black, with high boots and high collar with fish bones that were fashionable a hundred years ago. Well, Granny sat down next to the playpen, took out her knitting, and stayed put for the rest of the afternoon. From time to time she looked at her watch and gave me an order, such as: "Put him on the musical chair!" or "Put him on the potty!" or "It's time for his bath."

After I had given Johnny his bath, the cook came. "Now I will show you how to get him ready for his supper." She put something like a cellophane coat with long sleeves on him, on top of that a bib out of terry towelling. After his meal, Johnny was taken into the living-room, where the chairs and tea-table were moved out of the way. Johnny was to walk. The adults (father, Granny and the cook) formed a big circle, with Johnny standing in the centre. With their arms stretched out towards him they all said: "Walk, Johnny! Johnny walk!" They were all ready and eager to catch him in their arms, but Johnny just stood without moving. He must have thought: "If walking is so dangerous, I'd better not start it." After I had visited the mother in the hospital twice, I encouraged her to come home, which she did. I stayed on another four weeks, and now we, the mother and I, took care of Johnny. She was eager to follow my suggestions, and by the time I left, Johnny ran all over the house, talked well, and mother and child had a good relationship.

———

I have often been amazed by parent-children relationships. There was the family in California, where I had arrived to take care of a new baby and Gerda, the baby's sister. The atmosphere in the nursery was relaxed and pleasant until four-year old Gerda dropped the tray with the plasticine; it just slipped out of her hand. There it was now, on the floor, just as she was about to sit down and play with it. Gerda stood there, petrified. "Just pick it up", I said. No sooner had I said it than Gerda's mother called me from the next room. I went to see her. "No, Miss Karger, don't tell her to pick it up. She must not pick it up, not now. Gerda has pick-up time every night at 7.00 pm, before she goes to bed. Then she has to pick everything up from the floor, only then!"

———

In another of the families where I worked as a maternity nurse there were two other children, 2-year old twins. They were healthy, active, lively children, but kept in their cot most of the day. Every evening, when their

163

father came home from work, he was told by his wife: "Give the twins what is owing to them", and the children, each in turn, were taken out of the cot and got a good spanking. The father told me: "I have to believe it if my wife tells me that they were naughty." At the beginning of this century, it was still the case that young children were threatened: "If you don't behave, the policeman will get you", or: "Wait till Daddy gets home." Children were often sent to bed as a punishment, so that they came to regard bed as a bad place, and made a fuss about being put to bed at night.

———

Children sometimes find themselves 'caught' between two adults. There was 3-year old Eberhardt, a sturdy, independent and healthy child. When his mother enrolled him in my nursery school, she said: "Be very strict with him; he is naughty and stubborn." I found him friendly, cooperative and nice; no problem at all. He always came to school by himself, but one morning he arrived in tears. "What happened?" I asked. "I didn't want to come today", he said. "Do you want to go back home?" I asked. That made him cry even more. "Mummy would just send me back again. I don't want to walk back and forward all day!"

———

Sometimes I have been taken unawares by children's approach to life. There was Betty, a 4-year old, whose governess I was, and whose mother was German. One day the mother said something to me in German, and Betty said: "Mummy, it isn't polite to talk in a language that someone else in the room doesn't understand." Her mother replied: "Ask Miss Karger to teach you German. Then you'll understand all that I say." "Much good that would do me", said Betty angrily. "As soon as I understand German you would talk to her in French!"

There was another 4-year old who told me: "Miss Karger, you know what I would like to do?" "What?" I asked. "I would like to take a big, big ladder which reaches all the way up to the sky." "And then?" "Then I would take you by the hand and walk with you all the way up to the top." "And then?" "Then I would take you to God, and ask him to make you as nice and black as I am!"

———

Rolf and Peter were 10 and 12. Their mother was a doctor and not at home during the day. When the long school holidays started she begged me to take the boys into my nursery school. Reluctantly I agreed to give it a trial, but it worked out alright; the boys became my helpers in the morning, and in the afternoon they joined the group of 6-12 year olds. Some months later I was invited to their house for dinner. A lively conversation was under way, and their mother was astounded that the boys talked to me so freely, not showing that formal respect that was customary when addressing a teacher. "Boys", she said, "You cannot talk like that to Miss Karger. She is your teacher! She is a lady." "Oh no", said the boys, "She is not a lady. She is our friend."

———

As children get older, their relationships with parents aren't always easy either. I was on a course in Parent Education run for those social workers and teachers who promised to start such a course in their own neighbourhood after they had attended this one. Being the director of a large day nursery for children of working mothers, I was eligible for this course. Mr Davies, one of the tutors, was the headmaster of a state school with the reputation of being very modern and progressive. In our first session, Mr Davies said: "One can have very good ideas in theory, but in practice it might be very different. I will give you an example from my own experience. When our son was eleven years old, my wife and I thought that we ought to instruct him about the facts of life. 'Helen', I said, 'Talk to Junior about it.' 'Why me?' said Helen. 'Because you are his mother', I said. 'But you are his father', said Helen.

We looked at each other, we two professional teachers, and then we decided that we should get him a good book on this so delicate yet so important subject. With the book under my arm, I casually went in to Junior's room. My son was stretched out on the floor, reading. 'What are you reading?' I asked him. 'Oh, this is a very interesting book about Indians.' 'David', I said, 'When you are finished with that book, I'd like you to read this one, and if there is anything that you do not understand, you can ask me.' Well, we waited one, two, three weeks. Our son never mentioned that book. Finally I asked him: 'By the way, David, have you read that book which I gave you some weeks ago?' 'What book? Oh, yes, that one. Yes, I read it.' 'What did you think of it?' 'I can't understand how anybody could have wanted to write such an uninteresting book', said David. 'Is there anything that you didn't understand, anything that you would like to know?' 'Yes, Dad. How does an incubator work?'"

"You see my point?"

CHAPTER 13

ART, PAINTING AND POETRY

I HAVE ALWAYS HAD a powerful impulse to express myself through art. I was once asked by an art teacher why I painted, and I replied: "Why do the birds sing?" The story of my painting began when I met Hilda in a sanatorium in Sydney, Australia, where I had been living for a year. She and I went on vacation together, and the first morning, after breakfast, Hilda came in with her knapsack and all her painting materials inside. She said: "You can come along with me, but you must not talk to me." I watched her paint, and a terrific urge came over me. 'I want to paint also', I thought.

The next day I told her this, and added: "But I have no materials." Hilda was a professional landscape artist with a charge account, so she sent off for some materials for me: oil paints, paper, brushes and turps. We went into the forest every morning after breakfast, and sat there, painting. The strange thing was, every day when it was time for lunch, Hilda always had a nice landscape, with each group of trees painted exactly where they were, and I had abstract designs.

One day I forgot the palette, but I took off my sunglasses and put them on a rock and used them as a palette, and that day I painted nice big sunglasses with different colours in them. One day I cleaned the brush in turps on my sandwich paper, and when I looked at it, it looked like a dog. I did a few more lines, and it <u>was</u> a dog, looking at me eagerly.

Some time later I saw an advertisement for paintings to be entered in an art exhibition. There was no entrance fee. I had never exhibited before, but thought I would put the dog in, so I framed it. In the catalogue you have to give the artist's name, and the title and price of the picture.

For the title I chose: 'The neighbour's dog'; it looked as if it was about to jump up at you. I had no idea how to price it; if I made the price too high, people would think: 'She's crazy.' If I put it too low, people would think: 'She doesn't think much of her painting.' So I put on it: 'Not for sale'. I also put in a second picture, an abstract design.

When I arrived at the exhibition I found it was in a very exclusive house. I didn't want to go in, so my friend said: "After this long journey? I will take them in." My paintings were accepted, and I got an invitation to attend the preview. The mayor opened the proceedings with the news that they had received over 300 paintings, but only had room to hang 125. I went into the house, and there was my dog in the first room, painted on my cheese sandwich wrapper, and in the second room was my abstract fireside painting. It was a most exciting feeling; I was nailed to the floor. People came in and I heard them discussing my painting. There was a mother and daughter. The daughter said: "That's interesting." The mother said: "I wouldn't want to hang that in my bedroom."

The exhibition went on for two weeks, and then I went to collect my paintings. A gentleman approached me. "Why isn't your dog for sale?" he asked. "Are you interested?" I said. "Yes, very much so. You have only to tell me the price." I told him to give me a phone call, and I would then tell him whether I wanted to sell it or not. Then I asked the Secretary who the man was, and she said it was the town's Chief Librarian. I thought this was a good omen; I would sell it to him. When he rang me, I said: "I will sell it under one condition: you have to put a price on it." He suggested $4, the equivalent of a week's salary for me at that time.

I did another painting on my lunch wrapper, which I still have. Hilda and I were arguing one day, when I was supposed to be packing up my art things. I did it quickly and held it up to Hilda and said: "This is you!" It went into several exhibitions under the title 'A Friend's Portrait'.

———

In 1949 I joined Adult Education classes in Sydney and met John, a young, enthusiastic and encouraging person. There were only two courses offered: Beginners and Advanced, but I was determined to stay in his class, so having completed the Beginners, I booked in for it a second time. The office sent me back my cheque, saying that the class was full.

When the new term started, I went along anyway. I entered the class-room and to my surprise I found that the 24 other old students had done the same thing. When John entered the room, he found 25 new students sitting at the tables, and 25 old students standing round the walls.

"Well", he said, "Let me see if I can find a larger room." So for the next semester we all painted with John again, but as it was not an official course, we old students did not have to pay any fees. That was John — he just could not throw us out. At one of his first evening sessions, John demonstrated how to paint a landscape. Then he said: "Now take a large sheet of paper and paint a landscape. Has anybody any questions to ask?" I raised my hand: "Are we supposed to imagine a landscape in our mind, and try to put that on paper, or are we supposed to just let the paintbrush go ahead and follow the paper, letting it do what it wants to do?" "That is what some artists do", said John, and I became one of them. Later, on his recommendation, I was accepted into the Contemporary Arts Society of Sydney.

———

Sydney Adult Education offered excellent courses, and one of them was a 10-day residential seminar. There were 60 participants, and we were invited to sign up for any two out of the four activities on offer: paint-ing, sculpture, writing and music. "If you cannot paint, make the Painting Group your first choice", we were told. "If you cannot sing, make music your first choice." John led the Painting Group, but he allowed me to join as he realised that I had an educational interest in his method of teach-ing. It was marvellous. Here were 15 grown-up people who were con-vinced that they could not paint, or even draw a straight line. When they had booked for this course they had had no idea what they were in for.

On the first day each of us was handed a sheet of old newspaper. "Don't read it", said John, "Just colour in the different columns. You may change their shape a little bit by making the columns longer or shorter." On the second day: "Just doodle and see what comes out. Look at your paper from all sides and see if it suggests something." On the third day: "Fill the whole paper with bottles; any kind of bottles." On the fourth day it was a different approach again, and so it went on for 10 days. The words 'painting' and 'drawing' were never spoken; everyone was happy and busy, and the results were marvellous.

169

1991

ILKA

'The Argument'

8/7/94

ᴸKA

'Puppets'

171

'What now?'

1993

'Christopher Robin'

I had gone into my other group, the music group, very much *contre coeur*, against my conscience. As a child of eight I had been told by our singing teacher at school, who was also the organist of a big church in Berlin: "You cannot sing. Sit on the last bench, and do not sing!" That had been my musical education, yet I soon became very enthusiastic about our instructor and the way he led us into singing very lively folk-songs. After eight days I even composed a little song, although I could not read any musical notes. I sang my song to the instructor and he wrote the music out for me.

Every one of the four groups was very succesful, as the exhibition at the end of the seminar showed. We had come to realise that there is a creative instinct in every person, though unfortunately sometimes this creativity is crushed in childhood.

———

Then there was an instructor whose Saturday morning class in oil painting I had joined. For week after week I did the same thing: nothing. I stood in front of my easel, the paintbrush in my hand, but could not make myself put it down onto the canvas. Finally the instructor questioned me: "Why don't you paint?" "I cannot paint here." "Why not?" "I need a nice quiet atmosphere." "Is it not nice and quiet here?" "Yes, too quiet, like a churchyard. When I look around me, I feel that nobody looks happy, nobody looks relaxed, everybody seems to paint under a terrific strain. I cannot paint here."

———

Harry was different again. Harry put up a still life for me and said: "Sketch that with charcoal, then put the paints in as you see them." After I painted for a while, Harry came, took my paintbrush, and dipped it into some paint, but before he could get it down onto my canvas, I yelled at him: "Don't dare to touch it! It's my painting, not yours. Explain what you want me to do but don't do it for me!" In that same studio once, the student behind me said: "Harry, Harry, look what Ilse is doing." Harry asked: "What is she doing?" "She is putting the paint on the canvas." "Where else should she put it?" he said. Well, I was not putting the paints on to my palette to mix them, but put them straight on to the canvas and blended them while my landscape evolved at the same time. That way I could keep my eyes on my canvas without any interruption.

When we think of 'art' we usually think of the different branches. In reality they all belong to one big family, the family of 'expression'. There are many different branches, such as music, dance, sculpture, drama, painting and poetry. Each of them speaks and can express the same thing. Music can talk of joy, a painting can express joy. So can a sculpture or a stage play. All art expresses feelings. All art has rhythm. All art has form. All art has strength. All real art is honest. All art grows from within: you cannot separate the dancer from his dance - they are one! The painter does not paint 'pictures', he expresses his inner self. He paints because 'it' makes him paint. It is his way of talking, of breathing, of living. You cannot say to a bird: "Don't sing." Singing is a part of being a bird. All life is moving. It never stands still.

———

'The new day is just awakening in front of me. The birds are singing it in. The trees on the hill are still a quiet grey. But a soft orange is getting up from the horizon; it is spreading out in size, getting stronger in colour also, and the sky is now a light blue. Nature, the biggest painter of all time, mixes and blends her colours right on her big canvas while she is painting her landscape. Now the orange has become a pale yellow and the blue of the sky a light purple. What a privilege to watch nature at work. A perfect picture at every stage! My watch says 5.40 now. The sun is just rising. It looks like a golden ball in the centre of a soft yellow cross. Never have I seen it that way! Ten minutes later: it is a yellow half ball with horizontal yellow lines making a pattern through a large cloud.' (*From an entry in my diary*)

———

Now that my eyesight is failing, I paint out of the subconscious, almost like transcendental meditation. I'm now restricted to charcoal and pastels because I can't see the colours. I'm having to learn again how to handle the paints. When I feel like I want to do something, then I do it. A bird is not told when to sing. I'm restricted in my activities since my eyesight worsened, and painting is the only expression that is left to me. Sometimes I intend to draw something in particular, but most of the time I make movements with the charcoal and then I look at it. What does it suggest? And then I trim it up; could this be a nice group of people? I give it some emphasis to be something. Whatever it suggests to me, I make it into that, and that is how I paint: spontaneously.

175

Since poetry is also an important form of art for me, I have felt it right to include some of my poems, which have already appeared in 'Loose Leaves'. The original titles and illustrations have been retained.

—

Letter from Hobart to a friend in New York, 1968

Ruth: Our letters have met in mid-air. I let them speak for themselves:

"Are you coming or going?"
"I am coming and going."

"From where to where?"
"From there to there."

"From one land to another land?"
"From a Friend to a Friend"

"But why call them two countries, I ask you, why,
When there is just one heaven, and there is but one sky.
And there is but one sun. And there is but one moon.
We will be one world! I wonder how soon?"

Snowflakes

Have you ever watched a snowflake when it has just fallen on to your coat?
    A superb piece of art.
    So delicate! So symmetrical!
    And a minute later, it's gone.
    Where did it go?
It came and it went.
We all come - and we all go!
From where are we coming and where do we go?
    Do you know?

The Friendship Tree - Sydney, Australia, 1967

And they took some seeds
And planted a tree
And the seeds were
    Loving care and sympathy.
And the tree bears fruit
And the fruits you can see
Are Contentment and Peace
    and Harmony.

Advice to a Friend

Go to bed before you are dead tired
    and then look at the word '*FREUDE*' (Joy)

        Look at it! Smile at it!
        Let it look at you; let it smile at you.

        Feel it! Let it warm you.

With its warmth on your heart,
With its kiss on your face,
    let yourself fall
        into heavenly sleep.

Pendle Hill - Pennsylvania, USA, 1968

What is Pendle Hill?
There is no word that can explain,
I searched and searched - but all in vain!
I walked around in all its grounds
And what I saw and what I found was beautiful.
But still: it's not the heart of Pendle Hill.

What is Pendle Hill?
Is it a mood? An atmosphere?
A place of rest? A place of peace?
A meeting place for lonely people?
A seminar for active living?
A mutual place for 'take and giving'?
Is it a place for education?
Is it a place for contemplation?
What is the key to Pendle Hill?
What is the language in Pendle Hill?
A friendly smile and a warm handshake.
It does not take words to communicate.
All people all over the world understand
A friendly face and a warm handshake!

What makes Pendle Hill?
Sometimes you wonder and you think.
I sat in silence and I prayed
'God, let me know what's Pendle Hill,
Created and guided by your will.'
And the answer came to me last night.
It pierced the dark night and was light:
Pendle Hill is strength and truth and love!
Carry it with you wherever you go
If you want Pendle Hill to live on and to grow!

The Riddle 'I'

A letter? A word? A person?
Who? What? Where? Why?

So short, yet so important;
    that little big 'I'.

178

My Hat - the Panama

They killed my hat!
It's hard! It's flat! It's dead!
It was a beautiful hat!

It must be "shaped" they had said.
I say: "They were mad."
They put it "in form" they said.
You can see: it is dead!
They killed my hat!
 and that is that.

Joy

What is Joy?
What is it for?
Where does it come from?
And where does it go?
 Is it a plant?
 Is it a star?
 Is it nearby — or is it far?
Joy is priceless.
 You cannot buy it.
 You cannot hunt it.
And yet
 You can give it!
 You can receive it!
Joy speaks in many languages.
Joy is warm but never burns you.
Joy is bright but never blinds you.
Joy shines also in the dark.

Sleep

What is Sleep?
It's a present, a heavenly present.
Meet it with outstretched arms and it will embrace you most
        tenderly.
Sleep is quiet and understanding, it's soothing and reassuring.
Sleep is a good friend!
A friend to all.
        To the poor - and to the rich.
        To the sick - and to the healthy.
        To the young - and to the old.
        To all!
At the entrance door to Sleep
        you take off and leave behind
        your worries, your troubles,
        your pains and your sorrows.
            In the arms of Sleep
            you may rest
                and feel free!

The Open Door - Cologne, Germany, 1970

I met them at the 'Open Door'
'The Open Door', that is the place
Where people really come to face
Their brothers as they are.

Those are the products of their world around.
Those tread with others on a common ground.
They know Love, Dignity and Faith no more,
They feed on Hatred
But still they find: The Open Door.

The Open Door can mean a lot.
It is the place where they can face
Themselves and all the others.
And some discover after all
That 'all men can be brothers'.

(See Chapter 8)

The Light

This is the light which showed the way;
This is the light which made me stay;
This is the light which shines all day;
This is the light which made me say
    Thank you!

Thank you, you light from heaven;
Thank you, previous light
Which shines for everybody;
Which shines in day and night
    Thank you
    Divine light!

Dec. 1994

ILKA

182

CHAPTER 14

GEISTESGEGENWART

AND PEAK EXPERIENCES

THERE IS A WORD IN GERMAN, *Geistesgegenwart*, for which there is not really an equivalent word in English. A literal translation is 'the spirit's presence', meaning presence of mind. You cannot learn to acquire *Geistesgegenwart*, you are born with it if you are lucky. It has stood me in good stead in my life and work, as the following examples show.

The first instance was when I was on holiday with Betty (*who is mentioned in Chapter 3*). We were staying by the coast, and went for daily walks along the shore. One day we were standing on one of the break-waters, and Betty jumped off into the sand. I saw her sink in. Her feet disappeared. Her body disappeared. Further down she went. I threw myself down onto the sand, flat on my stomach. Now I was behind her. I grabbed her by the collar, pulled her out, and pushed her towards the shore. Wet, cold and exhausted, we returned to the hotel. The next day, the hotel manager told me: "There is a lot of quicksand here. Good thing that you acted so fast. A minute later and the sand would have closed over her head. Her body would never have been found."

Another example was Sammy, the only child in residence with 80 day-children. Sammy was in bed recuperating from an ear operation. I was busy in the room next to his when he called out, very joyfully: "Aunt Ilse! I have a gun, a real gun, with real fire!" I went to see. Sammy was sitting upright in his cot. His bed was on fire; there were high flames in front of him. I got hold of the burning blanket, carried it out of the room, and threw it into the bath tub. Sammy's sheets were scorched, but there was not a scratch on him. The big bandage around his head had not been touched. It was a miracle.

Then there were the three brothers aged five, six and seven, who were happy, healthy and lively children. I was their governess. One day the boys were playing upstairs, and I was downstairs with their mother. I said: "Excuse me; I'd better go upstairs." The mother said, "You don't have to go. It's nice and quiet upstairs." "Too quiet", I said, and went. The oldest boy was lying on the floor, his face white, and around his neck, a rope. His young brother was pulling on the end of the rope. "We're playing cowboys", they told me.

Another occasion involved Kay, a frail little girl, at Victor Maxwell House, the nursery school for blind children. Though totally blind, she was very agile, and a born acrobat. She loved to climb to the top of the 12 foot slide. Often she sat up there and sang before sliding down. And one day she jumped up in the air and did a backward somersault. I arrived just in time to catch her, and put her down on her feet. She lifted up her face towards me and said: "Miss Karger, I came down a new way!"

The opposite of *Geistesgegenwart* could be termed 'impulsive actions carried out under stress'. Sometimes the spirit seemed to have left me, as in the following examples where I acted stupidly. During the First World War, in the Summer of 1918, a group of schoolchildren were sent on vacation to Switzerland. At 16, I was the oldest child in the group. As a present for my mother, I bought a bar of soap and a reel of sewing yarn (we could not get real soap in Berlin, only an awful clay substitute). We had been told that we could not bring anything 'new' back into Germany. When our train stopped at the border for customs control, I got scared, and threw my presents out of the window. Three minutes later the German officials came into the train and said: "Who threw this soap out of the window?" But they did not give it back to me.

Another impulsive and stupid act happened when I was 60. I was going through some papers and came across my birth certificate. It did not look so nice any more — it looked old. The paper was curled and discoloured, so I tore it up and burnt it. Some months later I found I needed it again, so I wrote to my place of birth in Germany. They sent me a typed substitute, which confirmed that I was born on such and such a date, but I must say the old one looked better.

———

Of course, I have been in some difficult situations in my life which were not always easy to handle, such as those times when I have had to

184

appear in court. On the first occasion, an old friend of our family, Mr. Hamm, had taken my dog to the park. A policeman had issued him with a ticket, and told him that he must go to court to pay the fine for the 'offence', so I went to court with the ticket. I was ushered into a large room, took a seat amongst the other 'offenders', and waited for my turn. Finally the name 'Paul Hamm' was called out. I went to the front. The officiating clerk looked at me. "I wanted Mr Paul Hamm", he said. "I am Paul Hamm", I said. "You are not", the clerk said. "I am", I repeated. "You are not", said the clerk. "But it's my dog", I explained. "Your dog did not do anything wrong. It is Mr. Hamm who stood on the grass. He must be punished." I said: "He is an old friend of mine. I am glad to pay the fine for him." Finally, after some discussion, I was allowed to pay. "But be sure to have Mr. Hamm refund your money. We want him to be punished."

———

In the summer of 1947 I appeared in the Los Angeles Criminal Court as a hit-and-run-driver. My friend's husband Lenny, in whose old car I had had the accident, advised me: "At the trial, just plead guilty. Don't try to talk yourself out of it. And don't make jokes either!" The judge was facing me as I stood in the witness stand. He leafed through the papers referring to my offence, and then asked me: "Do you plead guilty?" "Your honour", I said, "I hit the car, but I did not run away. What happened was this. I was on my way home, and as I turned the last corner into my street, the door swung open. At the same moment I saw a truck coming in the opposite direction. As I closed the door, keeping only one hand on the wheel, I lost control and drove into a parked car. It gave me quite a shock. We sat there and discussed how this accident could have been avoided, expecting the driver of the hit car to come out of the restaurant in front of which he was parked. We were sure that he must have heard the crash. After some minutes, we drove one block further down our street and left our car standing in front of our house." The judge leafed through the papers again. Then, with a stern face, he said: "This is five days in jail or $50 — and considering the circumstances, I'll deduct $35." Happily I went home and told Lenny: "Never in my life have I made so much money in such a short time. Just for talking for two minutes I made $35."

———

I was involved in another court case in Los Angeles in 1947. The agency had sent me on a job with a new-born baby, where the maternity nurse had left two days earlier. I found the baby in a poor state of health,

185

a sick child with a second-degree infected burn on his knee. He was running a high temperature. As I found a scorched baby blanket and burned nappy in the nursery, my suspicions were aroused. The nurse was then questioned, but she insisted it must have happened after she had left. There had been two days between her leaving and my taking over, and the angry parents sued the nurse. I had to appear in court as the second nurse, and witness. It was not a pleasant job to confront another nurse, but I had to do it, and we won the case. I nursed that sick infant for six weeks.

I was in the witness stand again in York in 1974. On a dark and dull autumn day I was walking home from town. Home at that time was a bed-and-breakfast guest house. It was 5.30 pm and as I crossed a side road, I was knocked down by a car on the pedestrian crossing. I felt a terrific blow on my left thigh, and fell over. There I was, flat on my stomach, but not unconscious. I turned my head and looked into what seemed like two big yellow suns; the car's headlights. I thought: 'I will not try to get up. Let him come to me.' He came; a young man. I felt sorry for him. I did not ask for any compensation, though now after twenty years I still have a deep dent where the car damaged my muscle. He, on the other hand, made it into a court case by claiming that it was not on a pedestrian crossing. He had paid a smart lawyer to argue his case, and I had to confront a cross-examination, but they lost their case.

———

I also recall several natural catastrophes that I experienced. There was for instance the earthquake, which happened during my first visit to Los Angeles in the spring of 1947. I was in the chinaware department of a large store at the time, and felt a big jolt. I stumbled to the nearest chair, and no sooner had I sat down than everything around me seemed to tip over. China flew off the table with a big crash, people were shrieking and running in all directions, fire engines were dashing past and ambulance sirens were sounding.

I went home, and as I climbed the stairs to my furnished flat on the upper floor of the two-family house, I smelt something like burning rubber. I entered the living room; it smelled of smoke. I checked the kitchen, but could not see anything faulty. Finally I went to alert the landlady. "No", she assured me, "It's not in our house. Everything is all right." I went back to my living room. Over the wall, above the couch, there was a clay model of the head of a gypsy, with a scarf tied around the neck, and smoke was coming from the top of it. I looked behind the

186

couch, and at that moment a flash came out of the electric wire. How lucky that I had been in the room.

———

One catastrophe which affected me deeply, though I wasn't directly involved in it, was the big bush fire in Tasmania in 1967. I had arrived in Strathaven Lodge, Hobart, to be a resident in the Home there, and the fire was just about under control, but many lives had been lost, many people had been made homeless and penniless, and a large part of Tasmania's beautiful forest had been destroyed. My friend Margaret Wilkinson organised an aid scheme in the name of Quakers, and sometimes took me along on her visits to the victims of the fire. Her living room had been turned into a storehouse, a collection centre for donations of all kinds: clothing, bedding, furniture, crockery; people were very generous in making donations. Margaret gave help and advice in every conceivable way, and the morale of those victims was greatly improved.

There were other experiences also, peak experiences, which left such a deep impression on me that I have felt them all through my life. Even now, at the age of 93, I am still very much under their influence. The very first one was when I was six. A classmate of mine took me to her house to show me her new sister. As we entered the room, the mother was sitting in an easy chair, the new baby in her arms, which she was breast-feeding. I had never before seen such a small infant, or a baby drinking from its mother's breast. The young mother looked at her baby lovingly and happily; I had never seen a person look so involved, so happy; happy beyond words. She didn't seem to notice us standing there, so wrapped up was she in the baby. Even now, after 87 years, I can see this young mother with her new baby actually in front of me, a picture of happiness, a picture of the closeness of mother and child.

Twenty years later, when I was a student nurse in Vienna, and had the opportunity to be present at the birth of a new baby, I again felt very much involved. I had been standing for an hour or two at the bedside of the young woman who was in labour. And when finally the baby was lying there on the bed just newly born, I was gripped by joy; I was so overcome by joy and happiness that I don't think the young mother could have been more involved than I was. It was like a wonder, all of a sudden to see there in front of me a new life, a new baby completely shaped, with nothing missing, a lively new life, as if fallen from heaven as a present. That too was one of the peak experiences in my life.

1/4/93

ILKA

'Mother and Child'

New life in nature also excites me. Every spring when I see the first crocuses in the garden I am full of joy and happiness, and every new flower, when the buds open and the flower unfolds, that is a lovely experience. Everything new, every new life, every young green leaf on a tree is big joy, a peak experience, a wonder, and I think it will always be so. Even now, at my age, I am still excited and happy about new life wherever I see it.

———

Another unforgettable experience occurred while I was a student nurse in a city hospital. I was on night duty in the infants ward. When the doctor made his rounds I went with him. As we came to Peter's cot, the doctor said: "He will not live through the night. Don't even call me for him. I can write out his death certificate tomorrow morning. But if you find spare time, carry him around." That night I carried Peter around for several hours, and mine was an unforeseen reward: a glance into a human soul. Here I was, a young student nurse, an agnostic who did not believe in the existence of a soul, in the value of religion. That night I saw a human life unfolding in front of my eyes. It covered the whole cycle of life — from beginning to end.

When I picked him up, Peter was an infant with the face and expression of an infant. While I held him he passed through all stages of life. His face and expression changed from a young child to an adult and then to an old wise man. There was no pain in his face - no doubt - no fear. He did not fight death. He seemed to know his way. He was very serene. He looked straight at me. It seemed that he wanted me to know what he knew. He understood, and he wanted me to understand too. Peter died in my arms. I closed his eyes and put him in his cot. 'Yes', I thought, 'This is not a broken-off life, nipped off in the beginning. It is a fulfilled life. Peter has lived his whole life.'

———

Another of the high points in my life was on the 14th December 1959. It was in the courthouse in Concord, New Hampshire, for the trial of Willard Uphaus on a charge of un-American Activities. We, a group of about 90 people, had assembled in front of the courthouse and there we conducted a Meeting for Worship half an hour before the trial started. Our Meeting was conducted first by a Methodist Minister, then a Rabbi, and for the last ten minutes it was a quiet Meeting for Worship in the Quaker way.

Some minutes before three o'clock, when we all ascended the stairs to the courtroom, we were stopped by a guard who told us: "The courtroom is full. You cannot get in." They had filled the courtroom with a class of school children so that we, Willard's friends and supporters, could not get in. Then I noticed Willard still standing outside the courthouse, talking, and I reminded him that it was time to go in. He walked up the stairs and was met by one of the guards, who yelled at him: "Stay down there! You cannot go in; the courtroom is full." Willard, in his nice, quiet way, said to the guard: "My name is Willard Uphaus", and the guard yelled at him: "I don't care what your name is, the courtroom is full. You cannot go in!" Willard said: "I think they need me up there - you had better find out."

189

Then the trial started, and we stood downstairs in the vestibule for three hours, singing hymns and carols just to show them in the courtroom that we were present. A reporter from the New York Post, who was upstairs in the courtroom, came down every quarter of an hour to tell us how the trial was going. Well, Willard was given a last chance to hand over the addresses and names of all the people who had been guests of World Fellowship that summer, but he refused. When he was asked: "Where are those addresses?" he pointed to a pocket of his shirt, and said: "They are right here, in my pocket. They are very close to my heart, and that is where they will stay."

After three hours Willard was sentenced to 12 months jail, and the sentence said: "As soon as you hand over those names and addresses to us, you will be free". But Willard did not hand over the names. When the verdict was announced, he was led down the big marble stairs, and as he came down with sheriffs at each side of him, we all started to sing the National Anthem, so that his guards had to stop. They stood there while we sang through all the verses, and then Willard waved to us and called out: "Keep up the good work!" While Willard was being led into the police car to be driven to the village jail in Boscaven, a group of us raced ahead in our cars, and when Willard arrived and walked from the police car into the jail, that group of friends again sang a hymn to him and wished him well.

Willard in his very strong character and his excellent inner discipline was a marvellous example for all of us through this year of imprisonment. We from World Fellowship, and other friends and Quakers who joined us, led by Willard's spiritual strength and leadership, really were able to support him. All through the next summer we went every Wednesday to Boscaven to picket the jail. We stood on the lawn in front of the jail, sang folk songs and hymns, and did folk dancing. We were led by Willard, though as he was on the top floor of the jail we could only see his raised arms. But still he conducted our songs, and after each song we called up to him: "What shall we sing now? What do you want to hear?" When, after three hours, we shouted good-bye, all the other prisoners behind their windows called down to us: "Thank you for coming. Come again. Come again!"

———

I have been a member of the Society of Friends for over 25 years, and have attended many, many Quaker Meetings for Worship. One stands out specially. As I remember it, the Meeting took place in a college lecture hall with a microphone and loudspeakers. We were sitting in the

190

hall, ready to start, when in through the door walked a group of black Africans, representing the Black Power Movement. These men, about 30, were all dressed in their national costumes, tall, and made very imposing figures. They walked into the Meeting hall and straight up to the clerk of the Meeting, and addressed him as follows: "Brother, will you get up and sit somewhere else, because we are taking over this Meeting now." The clerk and the elders quietly got up and found their seats amongst the other Quakers.

The leader then took the microphone and announced that over 300 years ago the black men in Africa were taken as prisoners to America and sold there as slaves, and they had been exploited and mistreated since that time. Now the time had come when the black Africans demanded from the white Churches a restitution for what had been done to them. They named a very big sum which they wanted. The Meeting went on silently; the Quakers were invited to comment, but no one said anything. Finally one of the Quakers addressed the clerk: "Will you please tell me in whose hands this Meeting is?" and the clerk, in a very quiet but firm voice answered: "This Meeting is, as all Quaker Meetings are, in God's hands". I was very impressed by the way in which the Quakers were led through this Meeting. There was no feeling of confrontation, no feeling of hatred. It really was a perfect Meeting, and at the end the black Africans shook hands with the Quakers and left quietly.

5/11/93

ILKA

CHAPTER 15

SPIRITUAL INSIGHTS

Religion

I HAD MY FIRST ENCOUNTER with religion when I was six years old. At school, a little girl pointed her finger at me and said: "My Mummy said that I should not talk to you. She said you are a Jew." At home, I asked my mother: "Am I a Jew?" "Yes", she said, "But it does not matter what religion one is. Every religion is as good or bad as every other religion. You don't really need a religion. Your conscience is your religion. What you can do with a good conscience, that you may do. You must not hurt another person, and what is holy to another person, that you must respect. You do not criticise it, and you must not joke about it."

There were three subjects that were never mentioned in our house: religion, politics and sex. Religion was not an issue at home, as we were free thinkers, but in school we felt discrimination. During the First World War, anti-semitism was very strong. Towards the end of the last year of the war, there were 41 pupils in my class altogether: myself, twenty Protestants and twenty who were Jewish. We were all girls, aged 16 and 17; it was like two opposing armies, and there were real fights. Hair was being pulled. Poor me; I stood in the middle in 'no man's land'. I was attacked by both sides. "Dirty Jew!" yelled the Protestant girls at me. "You are not a good Jew!" shouted the Jewish girls.

In my parents' house, locked behind a glass door in the book-case, was an old leather bible. It was never taken out of the book-case. As a child, and later teenager, I thought: 'The bible is such a holy book that one is not allowed to touch it.' As a young person I believed that I did

193

not discriminate, that I was on good terms with all religions, but that was not so. I hated all religions. It took me a long time to rectify that.

———

In Australia, while I was being interviewed by the Secretary of the Sydney Day-Nursery-School Association, I was asked: "What Church are you affiliated to?" My answer was: "None. When there is a Church for all people, then I will be affiliated to it." After having attended Quaker Meetings for many years, though, I joined the Religious Society of Friends (Quakers) in Hobart in 1967, and twenty years later I transferred my membership to York, England.

———

Often I have asked myself: what is 'Religion'? Is it God? Is it a relationship to God? Is it a relationship to nature - to everything in nature? A relationship to all the elements like sun and wind and rain, fire or water? A relationship to life and all that is alive? Is it a feeling, a feeling of being a part of it all? A drop in the ocean? A pebble on the beach? A tree in the forest? A link in the chain? Whatever we are, we are a part of something. And as that part we have to function. Only if each part is working correctly can the whole 'something' function.

———

There came a time when I felt that I had a relationship with God, and my feelings in regard to this relationship became very strong. My first spontaneous prayer one morning was:
Take me and shake me
and whirl me around,
and then put me down
with my feet on the ground.
I want to be taken
I am ready to be shaken
I am clay in your hands.

★★★

Pages from my Diary

After I had witnessed my first Quaker wedding, the following thoughts came to me: 'I have never seen them. I have not met them yet.

194

Today they will be married in the Quaker meeting house. They have been on my mind last night and even followed me into my sleep. I saw them quite clearly; not their outer appearance, but as two spirits joined together. There was no wedding party, no wedding-cake, no confetti. They did not seem overawed with joy. But they seemed to merge into each other. They knew that they were going to live together and for each other. They will help each other. They will support each other. They will strengthen each other, and together they will grow and walk through life. Wedding', I thought, 'I would like to see it spelt welding.'

———

One morning my thoughts were set on 'day and night'. I found that my relationship to 'day' and 'night' had changed. It used to be two opposites: night was dark, day was light; night was dead, day was life. Not any more. For me they had become one cycle, one whole. When I retire to bed at night, I do not any longer feel as if I am quitting, giving up the day. I feel it is like going home to calm and quiet and heavenly silence. "Here I am", I say, "Please take me in." And I have the feeling of witnessing the sunset of my own self. My physical self becomes so relaxed, so peaceful, so light , and then seems to disappear from the horizon. But I am still awake; I am watching this sunset, and it is a beautiful feeling. My spirit seems freed from the weight of my aching bones. Happily I put my spirit into the arms of the night, and it feels as if I'm living through the act of falling asleep. In the morning I used to fight against waking up. I did not like to face the day. Not any more; I wake up very gradually now, like the dawn; as if it's dawning inside myself. I feel as if I myself have become a particle of nature. I belong. I begin to feel that I belong to this whole big universe. I am not a stranger in God's world any more, not a tourist who came as a sightseer with camera and field glasses.

———

I don't know when it happened, I don't know why it happened, but lately I find it hard to wake up in the morning. I am in an in-between state between 'asleep' and 'awake' for what seems a long time. I would like to hold on to that in-between state or return to 'sleeping'. But I know that I have to go on and allow myself to wake up. I seem to need a lot of rest now, inner rest, and I wonder why. I seem to want to indulge in this 'in-between time', this peaceful time, when the body is still completely relaxed and quiet and I myself am awakening.

———

One morning I experienced something new: a precious time between night and day. I lay there, very very quiet, with my eyes closed, for two hours. My curtains were closed, and my eyes were closed, but I knew that it was dark outside ... and I appreciated the darkness, the stillness, the quietness around me, and the stillness and quietness inside me. My thoughts seemed to talk to me, very clearly and very outspoken, but not with any sound. I had a consultation or conversation with my inner self. We did not want the dawn outside to interrupt us. We wanted to be sheltered by the dark around us. We were as if in a nest; we felt safe and warm. And there was just enough light for us to see each other. It was not a glaring light. It was a candle light, a light which had life, and generated life. What did we talk about? Our words were thoughts. But our thoughts were so clear and strong that they seemed to be words. What were our thoughts? "We are a part, a particle of nature itself. We should not stand on the wayside and watch and admire nature as it passes by. We should be of it, and in it."

———

"Wake up!" This was said to me early one morning while I was still sound asleep. I heard it very clearly. It seemed to be a familiar voice. A full and melodic voice. It was firm but gentle. Though in the imperative, it did not seem a command. I tried to listen for more — and like a far-away echo I seemed to hear: "Wake up and be alive!" Then I woke up physically, and started to think. No, this was no dream, and it was not a human voice. This voice spoke only two words but with those two words said so much: "Wake up and be alive!" Will I be able to follow that call?

———

I have a new teacher! One morning, as I opened my eyes he was there: "You had a good night; you are relaxed; you are rested; you were waiting for me", he said. "Stay where you are, comfortable and still. Are you ready?" "Yes." "Will you listen to me?" "Yes." "Step out of yourself. Stand beside yourself! And now look into yourself." I lay there for a long time, looking into myself. Then I felt the day awakening outside, so I opened my eyes to the outward world. A beautiful day was in front of me, a sharp contrast to what I saw in myself.

———

This morning before dawn I tried to return to yesterday before dawn, but in vain. Yesterday did not return. I waited for a long time, but it did not come. And finally I caught on: my assignment had been given to me.

196

I have to pull out weeds. I have to loosen the ground and take them out very gently and carefully, or I might hurt the roots of the young shoot, my soul. The roots of my weeds might be intertwined with the roots of my soul, and the soul must be freed without being hurt.

———

I have just opened my curtains: what a dark sky! But in the upper right corner is a small white patch. 'Is it a snow-white cloud amongst the mass of black?' I wonder. And in the lower left there is a golden thread in the dark black. 'My sun', I think. 'There is my sun. Our sun', I correct myself, 'Everybody's sun.' In sun is warmth and friendliness. Who sent the sun into this dark world? What is its purpose? It is spreading 'light' outside in nature; before my very eyes, it's getting light. In half an hour it has changed from night to day. Yes, it is spreading light outside, but also inner light: it makes me reflect about inner things.

It is day now, outside; not a joyful, happy day, a grey day. But 'grey days' are also days of life. They also have their message, their challenge and their worth. Let me study this day. Let me learn from it. Let me be in it, and with it!

———

Something very beautiful has happened. All of a sudden I felt it: it feels like there is a little seed planted right in the middle of my very core. This seed is small, but very real and compact. It's a spiritual seed, composed of love particles, love received from different sources; unexpected, undeserved love particles which make up this embryo. I am now experiencing the joy of a mother when she feels the beginning of a new life inside herself. I am filled with joy and immense gratitude. I am trusted with a 'new life'. I will try to carry it to maturity, so that it can be born to become a living spirit. I can't remember ever having felt so relaxed, and so happy!

★★★

Dreams

I dreamt it was night. I was lying in my bed, comfortably relaxed, on my back. The door opened and I saw them: two tall and slender figures, dressed like nuns in long white habits, wearing white veils flowing down their backs. They looked very dignified. They kind of floated into my room scarcely touching the floor with their feet. With them they

197

brought in a long, white chest. They looked very friendly and calm. They smiled at me. They put that white chest on the floor in front of my bed. Now they stood side by side in front of my bed. Very gently they put their hands under my back and lifted me out of my bed. They lowered me down into that white chest. I was put on a soft quilt; it was snow-white silk material with lovely pink rose buds. The whole chest was lined with that white silk with rose buds, also the feather pillow under my head. They covered me with a lovely eiderdown and tucked it in so gently all around me. Then they looked at me lovingly and asked: "Are you comfortable?" "Yes", I said, "You can put on the lid. I will go to sleep." Then I woke up. It was 7.00 am, and an hour later I had my first heart attack.

———

I had a strange dream last night. Cläre was flying, floating, through the sky. It was a dark night sky, and Cläre was looking down, apparently looking out for me. Her arm was stretched downwards, her hand ready to catch mine as she passed me in her flight, as if to take me along with her.

★★★

Letters

Cläre: It was just wonderful; I mean, our meeting in the night. All of a sudden you were there! You looked so happy. No, we did not talk and we did not walk. We just <u>were</u>. We felt so alive; so radiant; so real. And it did not feel like 'you' and 'I'; it was 'we'; it was as if we had become one. In the morning, when I woke up, I was still filled with joy and happiness. I was elated.

I wonder, Cläre, did it come to the surface of your consciousness also, that our spirits really met while our bodies were sleeping soundly? And do not think that I was only dreaming, I was not. A dream feels entirely different. From a dream one wakes up suddenly, and in the moment when one wakes up, the dream breaks off. But this morning, when I woke up, you were still with me, only then you became your physical self, and I said: "Now let's get up, Cläre."

I wonder when our spirits will meet again in quiet togetherness. Cläre; dear Cläre. I am tired, and you do want me to say 'Good night'. I know you. I always say 'Good night' to you , but does it have to be with ink on paper? Do letters have to be written with ink on paper? The

198

spiritual language is so much deeper. Also, the spelling of it is simpler. The dictionary is not needed. Let's practise it. Much love, Ilse.

——

Margaret Wilkinson had a great formative influence in my life. She was a friend, counsellor and spiritual adviser to me. The following four extracts are taken from the many letters that we exchanged over the years.

Margaret: I need your help if you can help me with this. The problem is Isabel. No, the problem is not Isabel, it's me. But it is caused by Isabel — not really by her but by her age. Her age is haunting me. It even haunts me at night in my sleep. I seem ever so aware of her age: 86. And I know that 86 is followed by 87, and 87 is followed by 88 and so on. And I want her to stop getting older. I want her to always be as she is now: strong and active, physically and mentally, healthy and happy. I am scared of losing her one day. When I walk with her around the island I think: 'How much longer will she be able to do it?' When I see her digging in the garden, the same thought comes to me. I don't seem able to convert my thoughts in a better direction like: 'How beautiful that she is still like that at 86. So radiant. So active. So stimulated and stimulating.' Margaret, I am fretting when really I should be rejoicing! How does one learn not to look into the future when the future seems near and grey and foggy?

——

Margaret: Why is it that we can easily accept some people as they are, and find it so hard with others? Why do we approach some people more easily than others? Why are we so critical with some and not with others (the 'we' really stands for 'I')? And why do changes which come as a natural development hit us so badly? Why is it so hard to realise that everything and everybody changes all the time and never stands still? Why are we trying to catch a moment in someone's life and want to imprison that moment to preserve it for ever? My younger brother for instance is a man of 60 now, but I very often think of him still as the blond curly-haired baby. Why don't we let the past be gone and walk in the present?

——

Margaret: I have received your letter in which you told me about your mother's passing away. Margaret, never in my life have I heard of such a beautiful passing over. Such a perfect harmony of life and death. Such a complete harmony of the one who was leaving and the one who was left. Margaret, I am crying for joy. You did what only very few people, if any, could have done. It seems as if you took your mother beyond the very end door of life, right across the threshold of eternity. What heavenly peace must have been in your mother's and in your heart, to make that possible. You will never think of your mother's death as something terrible, not as an interruption of her life. You will think of it as a heavenly walk.

———

Margaret: It seems that my assignment now is to learn not to expect but to accept, and I expect this will keep me busy for quite a long while. In my mind I see my open paintbox. I have about twenty different colours. Yes, there is that strong clear blue. A beautiful colour. That brown there annoys me a little, though, but I don't expect it to turn into blue. And I know that it wouldn't improve if I mixed it with that beautiful bright blue. No, the brown would not improve; it would become muddy.

———

Dear Ruth: You asked me the other day to write down all the things which I would like best to do. I have thought it over, and it would be much easier to write down the things which I do not want to do. I do not want to conform to rules and regulations. I do not like to be confined in any way. I want to feel free, really free. What do I really want to do most? I do not know. Seagulls fascinate me. They seem to be floating on air without even moving their wings. Longingly I look up to the sky. I would love to be one of them. I also like to float on my back when swimming in a lake. It's a beautiful feeling to just lie completely still on your back, like a piece of driftwood, and be carried by the water. I just lie there on top of the water. I look up into the big, blue sky over me. Those drifting white clouds .... how I would love to be one of them!

When I walk through the forest at night, and there is the moon which greets me in such a friendly way, and some stars are sparkling so brightly, then — yes, then also I feel free. What do I want to do? Maybe I want to paint — just for the joy of painting! Or write — just for the joy of writing! I want to live for the joy of living! And I want to be loved in the same way as the grass and the flowers and the trees in the forest are loved, and the mountains. For no special reason, but just for being there. I want to be!

★★★

Thoughts on Life and Death

In December 1950 I was on my way to a seminar discussion, and I stopped over at my friend Margaret's house for three days. On the second day, all of a sudden, I became very restless inside. Then I started to cry, and could not control the sobbing. Margaret suggested that I sat down and painted. We both sat down and started to paint from our emotions. My painting turned out to be grief, deep grief (and as I write this 45 years later, my eyes fill with tears again). Eight days later I received the news of my mother's death.

The biggest blow, the greatest disappointment, the deepest hurt came to me on hearing of my mother's death. I was shattered. My greatest hope and desire had been to win mother's love. I had fought for it all my life, and now it was gone forever. And I think that mother felt the same. We wanted each other, we needed each other, but we could not reach out to each other, because we were too close to each other and stood in each other's shadow. We shared each other's unhappiness, we suffered together, and we could not support each other.

I believe that death is a very personal thing, and no one should interfere or intervene between death and the dying person. Give help if you can, but don't act as a brake. Don't try to hold the dying person back for selfish reasons. Let them go on. In the first part of this book I have written of the time when I was on the West Coast of America, and was called to my father's bedside in New York. I felt that I was racing against death. I hoped that I would get there in time to see my father, but all of a sudden I heard myself say: "Father, don't wait for me. If you want to go, go. Do not let me hold you back." Father went, and two days later I arrived in New York. I was very sorry not to have been in time, but I was also glad that I had not hindered him from 'going on'.

It seems to me that I can no longer define myself as a definite concrete subject. Maybe I have entered a new era in life, in which the physical part is more in the background and the spiritual and mental life starts to become more active. It seems that I am not just myself but am now also parts of several other people. Sometimes I catch myself thinking: 'This was not I but my mother in me, who said this', or: 'This was Heini's look which I used now', or: 'This was Günther, my elder brother, who smiled through me now.' And ever since I have had angina, I have the strong feeling of being very much Rudi, my middle brother. I see his face as my face, my eyes have become his eyes, my way of life is becoming his quiet way of suffering. He never complained. I will not complain either. I will just take up another trail in my way of life. There are so many different trails. They all can lead through some joy and happiness. Even if my feet cannot climb mountains any more, my thoughts can. If I cannot eat sweets any more, I can surely smell the sweet aromas in nature. My friend Margaret was so right years ago when she told me: "When one channel closes, another one opens up." I am experiencing that now; while my physical abilities diminish, my mental and spiritual abilities seem to be growing rapidly.

Looking over my whole life, I can see a silver thread running through it. It is intertwined with everything that happened. At times this thread was invisible, but it was always there, and it took me safely through more than 90 years. Everything happened, and I sat in my little nutshell and drifted along. Sometimes it was nice to be rocked by the sea; sometimes it was rough going. High waves rolled over me, the wind was strong and nearly turned me over, but I never perished!